Good Housekeeping
COOKING FOR CROWDS

Good Housekeeping
COOKING FOR CROWDS

RECIPES FOR EVERY OCCASION, FOR 6 TO 100

EBURY PRESS
LONDON

First published in 1995

1 3 5 7 9 10 8 6 4 2

First published in the United Kingdom in 1995 by Ebury Press,
Random House, 20 Vauxhall Bridge Road, London SW1V 2SA

Random House Australia (Pty) Limited
20 Alfred Street, Milsons Point, Sydney,
New South Wales 2061, Australia

Random House New Zealand Limited
18 Poland Road, Glenfield,
Auckland 10, New Zealand

Random House South Africa (Pty) Limited
PO Box 337, Bergvlei, South Africa

Random House UK Limited Reg. No. 954009

A CIP catalogue record for this book is available from the British Library

Research and recipe selection: Caroline Richmond Walker
Editor: Barbara Croxford
Design: Paul Wood

ISBN 0 09 180776 X

Printed and bound in Spain by Graficas Estella

Contents

INTRODUCTION

Parties are made for enjoyment and that goes for the host and hostess as well as the guests. However wonderful the food and ambience may be, few guests will be relaxed and happy if they see their hosts rushing about like scalded cats. So the first rule for party giving is careful pre-planning and organization. Remember that when cooking for crowds everything takes more time and space, from the shopping to the cooking to the parking of cars and hanging of guests' coats! The wonderful menus on the pages ahead can be used for a tiny crowd of six to a massive party of a hundred people. There are alternative quantity guides and 'vital statistics' for each menu but before you rush to the menus please first read all the advice given! A little reading now will save a lot of time and maybe heartache later.

PLANNING
YOUR PARTY

The first step - planning the menu

First of all decide on what type of party you want to have and whether it is feasible in the space you have available. A sit-down dinner for fifty people may sound grand until your guests are packed like sardines around skimpy trestle tables. In that situation it is far better to have a buffet party where fewer tables mean more space for people! Always think of the ages of your guests and what's best for them. Older people who find balancing plates and glasses difficult will prefer a sit-down meal, and it is certainly best if you can have a spot to anchor children. If they tear around with plates of food your house and carpet will never be the same again!

Now choose the menu — there are twenty on the pages ahead, ranging from brunches to teas to wedding receptions with ideas of others to prepare ahead and traditional recipes on pages 128 to 140. Seasonal menus are the best as food is cheapest and most readily available then. But do check whether you have any vegetarians coming or people with special dietary requirements whether religious or medical. And, of course, bear in mind the ages of your guests again; older and very young people usually prefer food to be quite simple whilst hearty young men will want something much more substantial. There's nothing worse than preparing a wonderful menu only to find that many guests have empty plates because they can't eat the food.

It may seem obvious but always budget the party before you start. The more formal the party the more it is going to cost!

Whilst selecting the menu, think carefully through as to how you are going to cook, store or reheat the food. Do you have big enough saucepans or casseroles to feed a crowd? And more importantly still, do you have space in or on your cooker to reheat these recipes? Friends may offer to lend you large saucepans or preserving pans which sound perfect until you find that only one can fit on the hob at a time. It is better and safer to serve a mainly cold buffet than a selection of lukewarm dishes which could well be breeding unpleasant bacteria as they sit in a warm room. Your oven too will only have limited capacity. If you cram it full of casseroles and dishes, the heat can't circulate properly and the oven's efficiency will be greatly impaired. Ask neighbours for the use of their ovens where practical. The problem of refrigerator space must also be considered. There will be wine bottles jostling for space besides heaps of salad ingredients, cheeses, cold chickens, cream and much, much more. Here your neighbours can be asked to help by lending you a shelf or two in their refrigerators.

And lastly, but most importantly too, when serving a buffet do make sure that all food can be eaten with a fork. There's nothing worse than looking longingly at scrumptious jacket potatoes which stubbornly refuse to be eaten with a fork!

Planning ahead

Once the menu has been decided upon make a careful time plan, this may sound pedantic but it saves all that last minute panic. Include on this all food and general goods to be ordered, the cleaning to be done, staff to be arranged as well as what to do 'on the day'.

- **Make detailed shopping lists, buying all unperishable items as early as possible**
  Don't forget tablecloths, napkins, candles, plenty of rubbish bags, foil, polythene bags, toilet rolls, etc. Sturdy paper plates are fine for cold food and plastic cutlery useful if no food needs cutting up
- **Order wines, beers, soft drinks, etc. and glasses (see below)**
- **Arrange extra help (see below)**
- **Hire tables, chairs, china and cutlery (see below)**
- **Book space in neighbours' refrigerators, freezers and ovens**
- **Order flowers if wished**

Extra help

Depending on the formality of your party, you may want to employ professional waiters and waitresses. Either contact them through your Yellow Pages under Caterers or Employment Agencies. Alternatively, most local hotels and clubs will help out in telling you where they hire their temporary staff. For less formal parties, friends, students or older children can be a great help but do give them clear briefs on their duties for the party. You just have to be bossy – a mass of well meaning friends wandering about chatting won't help the reheating of the casseroles. For a buffet meal one professional waitress can cope with about twenty-five guests provided that the drinks, salads, etc. are all help yourself. An untrained helper will find fifteen people sufficient to cope with. Book all staff early as all the agencies are busy, especially in the summer months.

Hiring equipment

Here again, look in your Yellow Pages this time under Hire Services for Catering Equipment Hire or Wedding Services. If there is no extra charge, order equipment a day ahead so you have plenty of time to unpack and check it out. Some firms will take equipment back dirty, this adds a bit to the cost but does save a lot of valuable time. Run through your menu ordering plates, glasses, cutlery and serving dishes as necessary. You may need jugs for water and fruit juice, ash trays, trestle tables and chairs and tablecloths. Don't forget coffee cups and saucers and even a coffee urn if you are catering for a very large number.

Refrigerators, freezers and hot cupboards can be hired too, but do check that you have sufficient power points to plug them in without overloading the system – a black out on the day of the party is not helpful.

The drinks

What drink to serve at parties is very much a personal preference, the important thing is not to run out! Many off-licences will sell wine on a sale or return basis which does mean that you can over-order just in case your guests are the thirsty type. Ask for advice for wines to suit your menu and don't be tempted by the cheapest available unless you want your guests to suffer from thunderous headaches.

We advise keeping the choice of wines to a minimum, this makes the filling of glasses much easier! Allow at least half a bottle a head, and order plenty of mineral waters, beers and soft drinks too. Many off-licences will lend glasses free of charge too – check when you order your wine. It is best to over-order on the glasses as inevitably guests put them down and can't remember where!

To chill large quantities of wine, line plastic tubs or rubbish bins with plastic sacks and fill with ice and water. Keep in a cool place. Ice can be delivered to the door (see Yellow Pages) or bought in off-licences. A 12.6 kg (28 lb) bag of ice should chill a case of wine in about 1 hour – allow longer on hot days. Remember to move chilled bottles up to the top as you put more bottles in. Still white wine can be opened ahead and the corks pressed gently back into the bottles.

Cooking in quantity

This is not just a question of quadrupling your favourite recipe and then letting it simmer or bake away. Liquids will not reduce at the same speed and cooking times may vary leaving you with a watery casserole or a sunken cake. Unless an experienced caterer we do not advise you to cook recipes for more than twelve people at one time. Few casserole dishes or saucepans will take larger quantities than this and if they do it is often difficult to ensure even heat right through. Just prepare food in smaller batches and chill or freeze for the big day. Never try and reheat it in too large a quantity in one batch either, it can take so long for the heat to reach the centre that the outside food becomes over-cooked.

How much to cook

The more people you are feeding the less you will need to allow per head. For a hundred people, 85-90 portions should be enough. This is especially true at buffet parties where the act of balancing a glass and plate is sometimes just too much to cope with. If you are offering a selection of main courses or desserts though, you will need to over cater a little as people like to 'taste' both. And if it is a 'treat' food like smoked salmon, everyone is bound to indulge so you must be generous. Refer to individual menus for more specific information.

Following the recipes

All the menus have countdowns or time plans but these relate to cooking the smallest quantity. Make sure that you allow yourself much more time when cooking for large numbers. And **most importantly** check that you have enough oven space; finding out on the day that you haven't only leads to tears.

Laying out a buffet

Have several serving points for the buffet food and the drinks too. This avoids bottlenecks and long delays. Ensure that plates, cutlery and napkins are set out at the start of the buffet table. Don't pile serving platters too high or food will spill over the table. It is better to replenish the dishes as necessary, especially with hot food. Have relays of food coming from the oven to ensure it is hot for all the guests. Keep cold food tightly covered until it is served and, if possible, add garnishes at the last minute too. They will look freshest then. Portion pies and gâteaux before the buffet starts or station one of the helpers to serve them out as guests often loathe to be the first to cut into them. And do ensure that there are some seats available for the elderly.

Handy hints

Make sure you have plenty of rubbish bags and drying-up cloths for the aftermath

Decide where to stack the dirty plates before the party starts. A kitchen overflowing with washing up looks unsightly and think about who is going to do the washing up

To save on time and energy, use good quality bought ingredients, such as mayonnaise, as a base for sauces and then add a few extra herbs or garlic to liven them up

Be ready for the occasional disaster such as a knocked over glass of wine. As it happens, mop the stain with cold water then top with several layers of absorbent kitchen paper. Stand on them until no more moisture will blot from the carpet

An electric carving knife is useful when slicing bread or creamy cakes

Make sure that candles, glasses and bottles are left on sturdy tables, well away from scampering children and pets

On the day, allow yourself plenty of time to cook or reheat food or to arrange platters of cold food. Always recruit plenty of helpers for this to avoid last minute panic

Consider where your guests are going to park their cars and if necessary inform the local police about the volume of traffic

It is a good idea to warn neighbours about the party – in case guests park in front of their garages or there is a lot of noise

Ask a friend or someone reliable to look after any pet which is likely to trip up the guests or devour the food

SUMMER WEDDING BUFFET

Celebrate a summer wedding or special birthday lunch with good friends with this perfect prepare-ahead party buffet.

Champagne Cocktails

Cheese Bites

Salmon Pithiviers with Herby Cream Sauce

Celebration Chicken

Golden Rice Salad

Cherry Tomato Salad

Peppered Leaf Salad with French Dressing

Lemon Fudge Tart

Sparkling Compote

Serves 20

An al fresco buffet is a delightful way in which to celebrate a summer wedding or other special occasion. You should always have a contingency plan in case of rain, however – either a marquee or an indoor venue large enough to accommodate all your guests. You may need to decide on the location as late as the morning of the party, so make sure that you have plenty of potential helpers standing by to help move the table around or put up an awning.

If your buffet table is outdoors, place it so that it is easily accessible from the kitchen and for the guests helping themselves. It will inevitably be the spot where guests congregate so there should be plenty of space on at least three sides. You may have to hire trestle tables (see Planning, page 9) so if you don't have a tablecloth large enough to cover it, think about using a large sheet.

Have a separate table for drinks, stocked with mineral water, fresh orange juice and your choice of wines and champagne. If you are short of refrigerator space, chill drinks in a large, clean dustbin filled with ice and half filled with water. Tea and coffee cups can be kept ready separately on trays.

Countdown

TWO WEEKS BEFORE
Make Cheese Bites and freeze. Make Salmon or Vegetarian Pithiviers to end of step 5, over wrap and freeze.
Make croûtons for Peppered Leaf Salad; freeze.

ONE WEEK BEFORE
Make French Dressing for Peppered Leaf Salad; chill. Make dressing for Cherry Tomato Salad; chill.

UP TO 4 DAYS BEFORE
Prepare Lemon Fudge Tart to end of step 4.

UP TO 3 DAYS BEFORE
Make Herby Cream Sauce. Cover and chill.

UP TO 2 DAYS BEFORE
Make pesto dressing for Golden Rice Salad.

DAY BEFORE
Soak fruit in brandy for Champagne Cocktails. Complete Celebration Chicken, cover and chill. Prepare Golden Rice Salad to end of step 3, cover and chill. Prepare Peppered Leaf Salad to end of step 2, cover and chill. Prepare Cherry Tomato Salad to end of step 2, cover and chill. Prepare Sparkling Compote to end of step 1, cover and chill. Thaw salmon overnight.

TO SERVE AT 1PM
9.30am Chill salmon before baking.
10.30am Thaw Cheese Bites and croûtons.
11.30am Preheat oven to 220°C (425°F) mark 7. Set out Herby Cream Sauce. Cut Lemon Fudge Tart into wedges, dust with icing sugar and chill.
12 noon Cook salmon.
12.30pm Assemble salads.
1pm Slice salmon. Add sparkling wine to compote. Complete cocktails

ALTERNATIVE CATERING QUANTITIES

(standard recipes serve 20)

Guests	50	100
Champagne Cocktails	x 3	x 5
Cheese Bites	x 2	x 3
Salmon or Vegetarian Pithiviers	x 2	x 4
Herby Cream Sauce	x 3	x 5
Celebration Chicken	x 2	x 4
Golden Rice Salad	x 2	x 4
Cherry Tomato Salad	x 2	x 4
Peppered Leaf Salad	x 2	x 4
French Dressing	300 ml (½ pint)	450 ml (¾ pint)
Lemon Fudge Tart	x 2	x 4
Sparkling Compote	x 2	x 4

VITAL STATISTICS

You will need lots of oven space here.

Salmon or Vegetarian Pithiviers

Make several Pithiviers in the sizes indicated as larger ones will be hard to fit onto baking sheets and even more difficult to slide off onto serving platters. Cook in rotation so that they are ready at slightly different times. (Make sure that you have platters large enough to take the Pithiviers.)

Lemon Fudge Tart

Portion this into smallish wedges as it is quite rich.

Champagne Cocktails

115 calories per serving

3 bottles of champagne

225 g (8 oz) small strawberries

175 ml (6 fl oz) brandy, preferably peach

30 ml (2 tbsp) caster sugar

mint leaves, to decorate

1 Chill the champagne in the refrigerator overnight. Soak the strawberries in the peach brandy and caster sugar overnight.

2 To serve, put a strawberry and a little liquid in the bottom of each glass. Top up with chilled champagne; decorate with mint leaves.

Cheese Bites

115 cals each   Makes about 100 bites

150 g (5 oz) butter, chilled

50 g (2 oz) Stilton or Roquefort cheese

50 g (2 oz) Cheddar cheese, grated

150 g (5 oz) self-raising white flour

salt and cayenne pepper

50 g (2 oz) walnuts, finely chopped

15 ml (1 tbsp) poppy seeds

1 Place the butter, cheeses and flour in a food processor with a good pinch of salt and cayenne pepper. Blend until the mixture comes together in a ball. Wrap and chill for 30 minutes.

2 Divide the pastry into two. Roll out each piece to 5 mm (¼ in) thick. Press the walnuts into the surface of one half and the poppy seeds into the other half. Stamp out 2.5 cm (1 in) rounds with a fluted cutter. (Knead and re-roll the leftover pastry as necessary and continue to stamp out more rounds.) Place the Cheese Bites on baking sheets.

3 Bake at 190°C (375°F) mark 5 for 10-12 minutes or until golden and firm to the touch. Cool on a wire rack, then store in an airtight container for up to a week (their flavour improves with age).

Salmon Pithiviers

420 cals per serving

125 g (4 oz) butter

225 g (8 oz) shallots, skinned and finely diced

225 g (8 oz) brown-cap mushrooms, halved and sliced

150 ml (5 fl oz) double cream or crème fraîche

225 g (8 oz) ricotta (see Cook's Tip) or goats' cheese

45 ml (3 tbsp) freshly grated Parmesan cheese

salt and pepper

900 g (2 lb) fresh spinach, washed

grated nutmeg

900 g (2 lb) puff pastry

2 salmon middle-cut fillets, weighing 700 g (1½lb) each, skinned

juice of 1 lemon

1 egg, beaten

Herby Cream Sauce

1 Melt 75 g (3 oz) of the butter in a frying pan and sauté the shallots until soft. Add the mushrooms to the pan and cook until the liquid has evaporated. Pour in the cream and allow to bubble until the mushrooms are just coated in the cream. Cool. Stir in the ricotta with the Parmesan. Adjust seasoning.

2 Melt the remaining butter in a large saucepan and sauté the spinach until the leaves have wilted. Drain and press out any excess moisture; roughly chop. Season with salt, pepper and grated nutmeg.

3 Divide the pastry into four. Roll out one piece into a square about 30.5-33 cm (12-13 in) or large enough to fit the two salmon fillets when put side by side. Place the pastry on a baking sheet and prick with a fork. Bake at 200°C (400°F) mark 6 for about 15 minutes or until brown. Cool and cut in half lengthways.

4 Place each piece of cooked pastry on a baking sheet; top with the salmon and trim around the pastry so that it is a similar size to the fish. Season and squeeze over a little lemon juice. Top each with spinach, making an indentation along the centre. Fill with the mushroom mixture.

5 Thinly roll out two more pieces of pastry, each one large enough to wrap around the fish with some pastry to tuck under the base. Brush with beaten egg. Using the remaining pastry to make a lattice pattern over the top. Glaze and chill until ready to cook. Glaze again.

6 Bake at 220°C (425°F) mark 7 for about 35-40 minutes. If the pastry gets too brown, cover loosely with foil. Stand for 15 minutes before serving with the Herby Cream Sauce.

Vegetarian Pithiviers

350 calories per serving

Roast 6 medium sized red peppers at 190°C (375°F) mark 5 for about 1 hour or until tender and well browned. Ease off the skins and slice the flesh into strips. Follow Salmon Pithiviers recipe, omitting the salmon and adding an extra 225 g (8 oz) goats' cheese in step 4. Layer the ingredients as in the basic recipe, adding an extra 225 g (8 oz) ricotta cheese and placing the peppers in the centre. Bake as for Salmon Pithiviers.

COOK'S TIP

If you can't find ricotta cheese replace it with curd or full-fat soft cheese.

Herby Cream Sauce

145 calories per serving

60 ml (4 tbsp) chopped fresh dill
60 ml (4 tbsp) chopped flat-leaf parsley
150 ml (5 fl oz) crème fraîche
300 ml (½ pint) mayonnaise
30 ml (2 tbsp) lemon juice
salt and pepper

1 Finely chop the herbs together. Mix with all the remaining ingredients, seasoning well to taste.

2 Cover the herby cream sauce and chill until required – up to three days.

Celebration Chicken

260 calories per serving

two 1.1 kg (2½ lb) smoked chickens (see Cook's Tip)
1 large cucumber
2 large ripe mangoes
grated rind and juice of 3 limes
300 ml (½ pint) vegetable oil
75 ml (5 tbsp) finely chopped fresh coriander
2 bunches spring onions, finely chopped
salt and pepper

1 Slice the chicken flesh into 5 cm (2 in) pieces, discarding any skin and bone. You should end up with about 1.4 kg (3 lb) of chicken flesh.

2 Halve the cucumber lengthways and remove the seeds with a teaspoon. Slice on the diagonal, then leave to drain on absorbent kitchen paper for about 30 minutes.

3 Cut down either side of mango stone. Cut away the flesh from the skin and place in a food processor with the grated lime rind and strained lime juice. Process until smooth. Keep the processor running and add the oil in a slow, steady stream.

4 Pour the mango dressing into a large bowl and combine with all the remaining ingredients, seasoning to taste. Cover and refrigerate for up to a day. Stir well before serving.

COOK'S TIP

Smoked chicken is available from supermarkets, and also by mail order. Alternatively use 700 g (1½ lb) smoked ham and 700g (1½ lb) cooked chicken.

Golden Rice Salad

185 calories per serving

450 g (1 lb) easy-cook long grain and wild rice mix
5 ml (1 tsp) turmeric
2.5 ml (½ tsp) paprika
30 ml (2 tbsp) oil
about 1.4 litres (2½ pints) strong vegetable stock
salt and pepper
8 spring onions, trimmed and finely chopped
200 ml (7 fl oz) French Dressing
20 ml (4 tsp) pesto sauce
900 g (2 lb) blanched mixed fresh green vegetables, such as broccoli florets, asparagus, sugar-snap peas

1 Place the rice, spices, oil and stock in a saucepan with a little salt. Bring to the boil, stirring. Stir and simmer for about 15 minutes or until the rice is cooked. Drain and rinse under cold running water.

2 Mix the rice with the spring onions. Whisk the French Dressing with the pesto sauce and seasoning, then toss with the rice mixture. Cover and refrigerate for up to two days.

3 Refrigerate the blanched vegetables in polythene bags. Just before serving, toss the rice mixture and vegetables together.

Cherry Tomato Salad

80 calories per serving

225 g (8 oz) mangetout, trimmed
450 g (1 lb) fresh peas, podded
salt and pepper
900 g (2 lb) red cherry tomatoes, halved
450 g (1 lb) yellow cherry tomatoes, halved
30 ml (2 tbsp) balsamic or sherry vinegar
120 ml (8 tbsp) olive oil
2 cloves garlic, skinned and crushed
10 ml (2 tsp) mustard powder

1 Blanch the mangetout and peas in boiling, salted water for 1 minute, then plunge them into cold water. Refrigerate the peas and mangetout in a polythene bag and the tomatoes in a covered bowl for up to a day.

2 Put the vinegar, oil, garlic and mustard into a jar with seasoning. Shake until well mixed. Store in a cool place for up to a week.

3 Just before serving, toss the tomatoes in the dressing and arrange in a serving dish. Sprinkle the peas and mangetout over.

Above: **Celebration Chicken**
Below: **Salmon Pithiviers** (page 15)

Peppered Leaf Salad

20 calories per serving

5 thin slices of bread
1 medium radicchio
1 bunch watercress
1 medium fine frisée
50 g (2 oz) baby leaf spinach
50 g (2 oz) rocket
250 g (9 oz) radishes
French Dressing

1 Using a heart-shaped cutter, stamp out croûtons from the bread. Bake or grill until golden on both sides. Cool; store in an airtight container for up to three days.

2 Tear the radicchio into bite-sized pieces; cut the stalks off the watercress; discard any tough outer leaves from the frisée. Wash all leaves in cold water. Drain and dry. Halve or quarter the radishes. Refrigerate the leaves and radishes in polythene bags for up to a day.

3 About 1 hour before serving, refresh the croûtons in a hot oven; cool. Toss all ingredients with a little French Dressing to coat.

French Dressing

105 calories per 15 ml (1 tbsp) Makes about 525 ml (18 fl oz)

200 ml (7 fl oz) olive oil
200 ml (7 fl oz) vegetable oil
125 ml (4 fl oz) white wine vinegar
pinch of sugar
pinch of mustard powder
2 cloves garlic, skinned and crushed (optional)
salt and pepper

1 In a screw-top jar, shake all the ingredients together. Season to taste. Store the dressing in a cool place for up to a week.

Lemon Fudge Tart

235 calories per serving

175 g (6 oz) plain white flour
icing sugar
265 g (9½ oz) butter
grated rind and juice of 5 lemons
10 eggs
275 g (10 oz) caster sugar
Sparkling Compote

1 Blend together the flour, 15 ml (1 tbsp) icing sugar and 90 g (3½ oz) of the butter in a food processor until the mixture resembles breadcrumbs. Divide between two 22 cm (8½ in) ceramic flan dishes and press into the base using your fingertips.

2 Bake at 170°C (325°F) mark 3 for about 35-40 minutes or until golden.

3 Melt the remaining butter for the filling and place in a food processor with the grated rind and squeezed juice of the lemons (about 200 ml/7 fl oz), the eggs and caster sugar. Blend until smooth, then pour over the warm shortbread. (The base must be warm when the filling is put in or the pastry crumbs will rise to the surface.)

4 Bake at 130°C (250°F) mark 1/2 for 1¼-1½ hours or until just set. (The slower the cooking time, the smoother the texture.) Leave to cool, then cover and refrigerate for up to four days.

5 To serve, remove from the refrigerator for 1 hour. Cut into wedges, ease out of the dishes and dust heavily with icing sugar. Return to the refrigerator until required.

Sparkling Compote

45 calories per serving

1.8 kg (4 lb) mixed summer berries
60 ml (4 tbsp) icing sugar
sparkling white wine, to serve

1 Pick over the fruits and place in a serving bowl. Mix with the icing sugar. Cover and chill for up to a day.

2 To serve, top the mixed summer berries with a little sparkling white wine.

Above: **Peppered Leaf Salad**
Right: **Sparkling Compote and Lemon Fudge Tart**

ANNIVERSARY TEA

There is nothing quite like a teatime celebration, especially in the garden on a fine summer's afternoon.

Sandwich Selection

Devonshire Fruit Scones

Hazelnut and Lemon Crisps

Lemon Sugar Biscuits

Cardamom Fingers

Blueberry Shortbread Tartlets

Tiny Eclairs

Strawberry and Passion Fruit Cake

Serves 12

The clink of china cup and saucer, pretty lace tablecloths and napkins and a mouthwatering selection of dainty savouries and sweets add up to an irresistible combination.

Even with twelve guests, preparing a tea need be no problem. Most of the basic recipes can be frozen in advance, leaving only the filling and decorating to be done on the day.

No elegant tea party is complete without a variety of dainty sandwiches. Start with crustless sandwiches, followed by scones and biscuits and, finally, a wonderfully delicious slice of real cream cake. Serve the more subtle teas — Darjeeling, Earl Grey, Lapsang Souchong — or herb or fruit teas, such as mango, with slices of lemon.

Countdown

A WEEK BEFORE
Prepare and bake shortbread bases and Hazelnut and Lemon Crisps and the Lemon Sugar Biscuits; store in separate containers.

TWO DAYS BEFORE
Make and bake Eclairs and Cardamom Fingers, cool, then store in separate airtight containers.

THE DAY BEFORE
Bake whisked sponge and scones; refrigerate in polythene bags.

ON THE DAY, TO SERVE AT 3PM
THE MORNING
Mix together strawberry mixture for cake. Keep in refrigerator. Make coffee and chocolate icing for eclairs. Make up sandwiches, but do not remove crusts (except sandwiches rolled into cigar shapes) or cut into shapes yet. Keep well wrapped in refrigerator.

1pm Fill cake – this will allow the flavours to mingle. Fill and top eclairs, warming icing and adding water as necessary. Fill tartlets, glaze if wished; sandwich hazelnut biscuits with lemon curd. Remove crusts from bread, cut into shapes and arrange on platters. Cover with damp greaseproof paper and cling film; chill until required. Arrange biscuits on serving plates. Place scones on a baking sheet; cover with foil and reheat to serve.

3pm Serve the tea.

ALTERNATIVE CATERING QUANTITIES

(standard recipes serve 12)

Guests	25	50	100
Sandwich selection (number of sandwiches)	100	180	300
Devonshire Fruit Scones	x 2	x 3	x 6
Cream/crème fraîche	600 ml (1 pint)	900 ml (1½ pints)	1.7 litres (3 pints)
Jam/preserve	700 g (1½lb)	900 g (2 lb)	1.8 kg (4 lb)
Hazelnut and Lemon Crisps	x 1	x 1	x 2
Lemon curd (optional)	450 g (1 lb)	450 g (1 lb)	900 g (2 lb)
Lemon Sugar Biscuits	x 1	x 1	x 2
Cardamom Fingers	x 1	x 2	x 2
Blueberry Shortbread Tarts	x 1½	x 3	x 5
Blueberries/raspberries	700 g (1½lb)	1.4 kg (3 lb)	2.3 kg (5 lb)
Tiny Eclairs	x 1	x 2	x 3
Strawberry and Passion Fruit Cream Cake	x 2	x 3	x 6

Tea   allow about 25 g (1 oz) for 12 medium cups
Milk allow about 450 ml (¾ pint) for 12 cups tea

FREEZER NOTES

Pack and freeze basic sponge, eclair cases, tartlet bases, scones and all biscuits, unfilled. Thaw biscuits and pastry cases on wire racks and scones and sponge wrapped in polythene bags. Complete as in original recipe.

VITAL STATISTICS

The most important thing to remember at a tea party is to keep all the food covered until the last minute to keep sandwiches fresh, biscuits crisp and cakes moist. Tent foil over eclairs to prevent it sticking to the icing.

COOK'S TIP

Vary shapes and types of bread and cut into small mouthful sizes. You will need to prepare about four sandwiches per person and keep them tightly covered to prevent them from drying out.

Smoked Trout and Watercress Pinwheels

40 calories per sandwich Makes about 48

½ large sliced white loaf – about 16 slices

50 g (2 oz) butter or margarine

275 g (10 oz) thinly sliced smoked trout or salmon

¼ bunch watercress, trimmed and chopped

lemon juice

freshly ground black pepper

1 Cut the crusts off the bread, then roll each slice with a rolling pin to flatten. Spread with butter. Cover with smoked trout, chopped watercress, a squeeze of lemon and plenty of freshly ground black pepper. Roll to form a cigar shape.

2 Wrap in greaseproof paper or foil and chill for about 1 hour before slicing into pinwheels.

Asparagus Rolls with Lemon Mayonnaise

65 calories per sandwich Makes about 32

15 fresh asparagus spears, thin if possible, trimmed

salt and pepper

½ large sliced brown loaf – about 16 slices

50 g (2 oz) butter or margarine

45 ml (3 tbsp) lemon mayonnaise

1 Tie the asparagus into a bundle, then place in a pan of boiling salted water, allowing the tips to remain above the water. Cook gently for about 4-5 minutes until the asparagus is just tender. Cool rapidly under cold running water.

2 Cut the crusts off the bread. Roll each slice with a rolling pin to flatten. Spread with butter and a little mayonnaise. Roll up each slice with an asparagus spear. Trim the end, cut in half to form two small rolls.

Cherry Tomato and Basil Triangles

55 calories per sandwich Makes about 32

50 g (2 oz) butter or margarine

½ large mixed-grain sliced loaf – about 16 slices

225 g (8 oz) cherry tomatoes, sliced

45 ml (3 tbsp) chopped fresh basil

salt and pepper

1 Butter the bread. Sandwich together with sliced tomatoes, plenty of fresh basil and seasoning.

2 Cut the crusts off the bread. Cut each sandwich into four neat triangles.

Cream Cheese and Walnut Rolls

65 calories per sandwich Makes about 32

½ large brown sliced loaf – about 16 slices

125 g (4 oz) full-fat soft cheese

50 g (2 oz) walnuts, chopped

salt and pepper

1 Cut the crusts off the bread, then spread liberally with cheese. Sprinkle over the chopped walnuts. Season. Roll up each slice to form a cigar shape. Cut in half.

Egg, Herb and Frisée Triangles

75 calories per serving Makes about 32

4 eggs, hard-boiled, finely chopped

60 ml (4 tbsp) mayonnaise

salt and pepper

30 ml (2 tbsp) fresh mixed herbs, such as parsley, chives

50 g (2 oz) butter or margarine

½ large sliced brown loaf – about 16 slices

a little frisée

1 Mix the eggs with the mayonnaise, seasoning and chopped herbs. Butter the bread.

2 Divide a little frisée and the egg mixture among half the slices of bread. Top with the remaining slices. Cut the crusts off the bread and divide each sandwich into four neat triangles.

Prawn and Dill Bites

80 calories per 'bite' Makes about 32

50 g (2 oz) butter or margarine

½ large sliced white loaf – about 16 slices

90 ml (6 tbsp) mayonnaise

salt and pepper

175 g (6 oz) cooked peeled prawns, roughly chopped

15 ml (1 tbsp) chopped fresh dill

1 Butter the bread. Mix together the rest of the ingredients. Divide among half slices of bread. Top with remaining slices.

2 Cut the crusts off the bread and divide each sandwich into four neat triangles.

Devonshire Fruit Scones

135 calories per scone Makes about 12

225 g (8 oz) self-raising white flour

25 g (1 oz) caster sugar

75 g (3 oz) butter or margarine

50 g (2 oz) dried mixed fruit

1 egg, beaten

milk, to mix and glaze

clotted cream, crème fraîche and jam or preserve, to serve

1 Mix together the flour and sugar. Rub in the butter until the mixture resembles fine breadcrumbs. Stir in the fruit.

2 Add the beaten egg and 45-60 ml (3-4 tbsp) milk to make a soft, but not sticky, dough. Knead lightly.

3 On a lightly floured surface, roll out the dough to a thickness of about 2 cm (¾ in). Use a 5 cm (2 in) fluted cutter to stamp into rounds. Place on a lightly greased baking sheet, brush each one lightly with milk.

4 Bake at 220°C (425°F) mark 7 for about 8 minutes until well risen and golden. Split and serve warm or cold with clotted cream or crème fraîche and jam or preserve.

Hazelnut and Lemon Crisps

50 calories per biscuit Makes about 52

125 g (4 oz) hazelnuts

125 g (4 oz) butter

50 g (2 oz) soft light brown sugar

25 g (1 oz) icing sugar

1 egg yolk

175 g (6 oz) plain white flour

lemon curd, to sandwich (optional)

icing sugar, to dust

1 Place the hazelnuts on a baking sheet and toast in the oven or under a hot grill until the skins loosen. Remove the skins by rubbing the nuts in a tea towel. Allow the nuts to turn golden in colour, but do not let them burn. Cool, then process or grind, preferably through a nut mouli, to a fine powder.

2 Soften the butter, add the sugars a little at a time and beat until very soft, pale and fluffy. Add the egg yolk with 15 ml (1 tbsp) water. Gradually work in the flour and prepared nuts until the mixture forms a smooth, pliable dough. Knead well to release the nut oils. Wrap and chill for 15-20 minutes.

3 Roll out the dough to a 3 mm (⅛ in) thickness. Stamp out rounds using a 5 cm (2 in) plain cutter. Prick lightly with a fork. Place on a greased baking sheet. Bake at 180°C (350°F) mark 4 for 7-10 minutes only–until golden in colour.

4 Allow to cool slightly before lifting onto a wire rack to cool. Store in an airtight container. Serve plain or sandwich the biscuits together with lemon curd. Dust lightly with icing sugar.

Lemon Sugar Biscuits

40 calories per biscuit Makes about 50

125 g (4 oz) butter

125 g (4 oz) caster sugar, plus extra for sprinkling

grated rind of 1 large lemon

1 egg white, lightly beaten

10 ml (2 tsp) double cream

150 g (5 oz) plain white flour

2.5 ml (½ tsp) baking powder

1 Cream the butter and sugar with the grated lemon rind until pale and fluffy. Gradually add the lightly beaten egg white, beating well between each addition. Add the cream with the sifted flour and baking powder. Mix until a smooth dough is formed. Chill for 30 minutes.

2 Shape the mixture into long rolls about 4 cm (1½in) diameter. Wrap in foil and freeze for 1 hour.

3 Cut the chilled dough into very thin slices. Place on a greased baking sheet, leaving room for the biscuits to spread. Sprinkle with caster sugar.

4 Bake at 190°C (375°F) mark 5 for 5-10 minutes or until golden. Allow to cool slightly, then carefully lift the biscuits onto a wire rack to cool. Store in an airtight container.

Cardamom Fingers

25 calories per biscuit Makes about 30

8-10 fresh green cardamom pods

50 g (2 oz) butter

50 g (2 oz) caster sugar

2 egg whites

50 g (2 oz) plain white flour

1 Split the cardamom pods. Crush the black seeds to a fine powder in a small pestle and mortar, or using the back of a teaspoon in a small bowl.

2 Soften the butter with a wooden spoon. Add the sugar and cardamom and mix well. Gradually add the unwhisked egg whites to the mixture, beating thoroughly after each addition. Lastly, lightly fold in the flour.

3 Spoon the mixture into a piping bag fitted with a 5 mm (¼ in) plain nozzle. Pipe the mixture into 7.5 cm (3 in) lengths onto buttered baking sheets, dusted with flour. Bake at 220°C (425°F) mark 7 on a high shelf for about 5 minutes or until golden and tinged with brown at the edges. Transfer to a wire rack to cool. Store in an airtight container.

Sandwich Selection (page 23)

Blueberry Shortbread Tartlets

150 calories per tartlet Makes about 16

125 g (4 oz) butter

50 g (2 oz) caster sugar

50 g (2 oz) semolina

125 g (4 oz) plain white flour

120 ml (8 tbsp) low-fat soft cheese

a little single cream

fresh blueberries and /or raspberries

redcurrant jelly (optional)

1 In a medium bowl, soften the butter with a wooden spoon. Add the sugar, semolina and flour and work together to form a smooth, pliable dough. Cover and chill for 20 minutes.

2 Roll out the shortbread to just under 5 mm (¼ in). Cut out circles using a 7.5 cm (3 in) plain cutter. Ease the circles into small brioche tins and prick the bases well. Bake at 150°C (300°F) mark 2 for 25-35 minutes or until firm and golden. Ease out of the tins and onto a wire rack to cool.

3 Mix the cheese with about 20 ml (4 tsp) cream to lighten the consistency. Spoon a little into the base of each tartlet. Arrange blueberries and/or raspberries on top.

4 If wished, glaze the fruit. Melt redcurrant jelly in a small pan, adding a little water if necessary. Allow to cool a little before glazing the fruit. Store in a cool place.

Tiny Eclairs

115 calories per eclair Makes about 24

Use a basic 2-egg choux pastry recipe (page 135), piping the mixture into small fingers. Fill with cream and top with chocolate and coffee icing. Store in the refrigerator until required. You will need about 300 ml (10 fl oz) double cream and 175 g (6 oz) glacé icing (page 135) for this quantity.

Strawberry and Passion Fruit Cake

350 calories per serving Serves about 12

white vegetable fat, for greasing

125 g (4 oz) plain white flour

4 eggs

125 g (4 oz) caster sugar

grated rind and juice of 1 orange

25 g (1 oz) icing sugar

450 g (1 lb) strawberries

2 passion fruit

600 ml (1 pint) double cream

1 Grease and base-line a 25 cm (9 in) cake tin, then dust out with flour and sugar. Sieve the flour twice and leave on one side.

2 Place the eggs, caster sugar and grated orange rind in a large mixing bowl. Use an electric whisk to whisk the ingredients together until the mixture is very pale and thick enough to leave a trail for about 5 seconds. Sift the flour again over the egg mixture. Fold in carefully using a metal spoon or spatula. Pour into the prepared tin.

3 Bake at 190°C (375°F) mark 5 just above the centre of the oven for 40-50 minutes or until pale brown and springy to the touch. Carefully loosen the cake from the edges of the tin using a palette knife. Turn out and cool on a wire rack.

4 Meanwhile, mix together the orange juice and icing sugar. Reserve about eight small strawberries for decoration; hull and quarter the remainder and toss lightly into the orange mixture. Cut the passion fruit in half, scoop out the pips and pulp, then add to the strawberries. Leave for about 20-30 minutes in the refrigerator to allow the flavours to develop.

5 Carefully split the cake into three horizontally. Whip the cream until it just holds its shape. Use to fill the cake with the drained strawberries and passion fruit.

6 Cover the top with cream, smooth over lightly and decorate with the reserved strawberries. Keep in the refrigerator until required.

Above: **Blueberry Shortbread Tartlet**

Below: **Hazelnut and Lemon Crisps, Lemon Sugar Biscuits and Cardamom Fingers** (page 24)

BIRTHDAY AL FRESCO LUNCH

Make the most of long summer days in the garden with our deliciously different, light buffet lunch.

Smoked Salmon Cheesecakes

Tossed Garlic Chicken

Pan-fried Courgette Salad

Mixed Shredded Salad

Summer Vegetable Platter

Easy Redcurrant Ice Cream

Easy Honey Ice Cream

Redcurrants in Port

Serves 12

Nothing is more relaxing than a lazy summer birthday lunch in the garden — and these are the ideal recipes to turn your buffet into a really special occasion.

The creamy savoury cheesecakes lightly flavoured with goat's cheese make a change from the usual flans, while the Tossed Garlic Chicken is a definite winner — along with the crunchy Pan-fried Courgette Salad. The Summer Vegetable Platter makes a stunning centrepiece for the table and it's light and healthy too.

The two quick ice cream recipes allow you to spend more time in the garden than in the kitchen, and they are a wonderful combination with the tangy Redcurrants in Port.

Countdown

ABOUT 3 DAYS BEFORE
Prepare and freeze ice creams. Make and bake pastry cases; cool and store in an airtight container.

THE DAY BEFORE
Fill and bake cheesecakes. Marinate chicken, cover and refrigerate. Wash, drain and dry a few radicchio leaves; refrigerate in a polythene bag. Prepare courgettes for the salad; refrigerate in a polythene bag. Slice almonds. Shred lettuce and spring onions for the salad; refrigerate in polythene bags. Prepare French dressing. Blanch or grill vegetables for platter. Cover and refrigerate. Prepare garlic dressing. Make port syrup and add redcurrants; cool, cover and chill.

TO SERVE AT 1PM
Early in the morning: garnish cheesecakes and glaze if wished; refrigerate to set. Cook Tossed Garlic Chicken, cool and cover, don't add to radicchio yet. Pan-fry Courgette Salad, cool and cover. Slice melon, cover and refrigerate.

ABOUT 12.30PM
Take cheesecakes out of refrigerator. Assemble and dress Shredded Salad and Summer Vegetable Platter. Slice bread to accompany buffet. Complete Tossed Garlic Chicken.
1pm Serve buffet. Remember to take ice creams out of freezer 10-15 minutes before serving so they soften.

ALTERNATIVE CATERING QUANTITIES
(Standard recipes serve 12)

Guests	25	50	100
Smoked Salmon Cheesecakes	x 1½	x 3	x 5
Tossed Garlic Chicken	x 2	x 4	x 7
Pan-fried Courgette Salad	x 2	x 4	x 6
Mixed Shredded Salad	x 2	x 4	x 6
(see below)			
French Dressing	200 ml	300 ml	450 ml
	(7 fl oz)	(½pt)	(¾ pt)
Summer Vegetable Platter	2.3 kg	4 kg	7.2 kg
(quantity of vegetables)	(5 lb)	(9 lb)	(16 lb)
Easy Redcurrant Ice Cream	x 2	x 4	x 7
Easy Honey Ice Cream	x 2	x 3	x 6

VITAL STATISTICS

Smoked Salmon Cheesecakes
For large numbers we recommend omitting the glaze and simply garnishing the flans with prawns and herbs. Cut up the flan into portions before serving.

Tossed Garlic Chicken
Unless you have many helpers and a huge frying pan for last minute cooking, it is best to serve this recipe cold. Don't overcrowd the pan when frying the chicken or it will stew rather than brown.

Mixed Shredded Salad
Choose a selection of leaves allowing about two medium heads for twelve people.

Ice Creams
Well ahead, scoop them onto baking sheets lined with greaseproof paper and return to the freezer until required. Serve straight from the freezer.

FREEZER NOTES
Pack and freeze baked pastry cases. Thaw for about 2 hours before filling and completing. Freeze ice creams as directed.

Smoked Salmon Cheesecakes

490 calories per serving

175 g (6 oz) butter or margarine
350 g (12 oz) plain white flour
90 ml (6 tbsp) finely chopped black olives
45 ml (3 tbsp) oil
350 g (12 oz) onion, skinned and finely chopped
225 g (8 oz) smoked salmon trimmings
4 eggs
350 g (12 oz) low-fat soft cheese
50 g (2 oz) soft, fresh goat's cheese
600 ml (1 pint) single cream or cream and milk mixed
30 ml (2 tbsp) chopped fresh thyme or dill
salt and pepper
7.5 ml (1½ tsp) powdered gelatine and 150 ml (¼ pint) dry white wine (optional)
To finish
125 g (4 oz) cooked, peeled prawns
thyme sprigs
75 g (3 oz) thinly sliced smoked salmon
few thin slices of lemon

1 Rub the butter into the flour. Stir in the olives, then bind to a firm dough with about 75-90 ml (5-6 tbsp) water. Knead lightly until just smooth. Wrap and chill for about 30 minutes.

2 On a lightly floured surface, thinly roll out half the pastry at a time and use each piece to line a 23 cm (9 in) fluted flan ring, about 4 cm (1½ in) deep, placed on a baking sheet. Alternatively, use a shallow 25.5 cm (10 in) flan ring. Chill well. Bake blind at 190°C (375°F) mark 5 until golden brown.

3 Heat the oil in a pan and cook the onion until soft and golden. Cool slightly. Roughly chop the smoked salmon trimmings. Whisk the eggs and cheeses together until almost smooth, then whisk in the cream, herbs and seasoning. Add salt sparingly. Divide the onion and smoked salmon between the cheesecakes and pour over the egg mixture.

4 Bake at 170°C (325°F) mark 3 for 50-60 minutes or until lightly set. Cool completely, then carefully ease off the tins.

5 To glaze the cheesecakes, soak the gelatine in a small bowl in 15 ml (1 tbsp) water. Dissolve by standing the bowl in a pan of simmering water until the gelatine liquifies and clears. Pour the wine into a measuring jug and stir in the warm gelatine, mixing well. Make up to 300 ml (½ pint) with water. Season well, cool, then chill until very cold, and on the point of setting.

6 Garnish one cheesecake with prawns and snips of thyme, and the other with a thin layer of smoked salmon, lemon slices and sprigs of thyme. Spoon over the glaze, if using. Transfer to the refrigerator and chill for 2 hours to set.

7 To serve, leave the cheesecakes at room temperature for about 20 minutes to take off the chill.

Tossed Garlic Chicken

155 calories per serving

75 ml (5 tbsp) soy sauce
75 ml (5 tbsp) lemon juice
45 ml (3 tbsp) soft dark brown sugar
oil
salt and pepper
900 g (2 lb) chicken breast fillets
2 bunches spring onions, trimmed
3 cloves garlic, skinned and thinly sliced
two 227 g (8 oz) cans water chestnuts
1 head radicchio
toasted sesame seeds (optional)

1 In a bowl, whisk together the soy sauce, lemon juice, sugar, 45 ml (3 tbsp) oil and plenty of pepper. Cut the chicken into strips, discarding the skin. Roughly slice the spring onions reserving the green tops. Add the onion and garlic to the marinade with the chicken. Stir well, cover and marinate in the refrigerator overnight.

2 The next day, thickly slice the water chestnuts. Rinse, drain and dry the radicchio leaves. Snip the spring onion tops. Strain the chicken from the marinade, reserving all the juices.

3 Heat a little oil in a wok or frying pan. Add about one-quarter of the chicken and stir-fry over a high heat until well browned and cooked through, about 3-4 minutes. Keep warm while frying the remaining chicken in batches, adding more oil if necessary.

4 Return all the chicken to the pan with the marinade, any remaining garlic and onions, and the water chestnuts. Cook over a high heat for 2-3 minutes, stirring frequently. Adjust seasoning.

5 Serve the chicken warm or cold on a bed of radicchio leaves sprinkled with spring onion tops and sesame seeds, if using.

Tossed Garlic Chicken

Pan-fried Courgette Salad

100 calories per serving

75 g (3 oz) blanched almonds
60 ml (4 tbsp) olive oil
700 g (1½ lb) each yellow and green courgettes, thickly sliced
45 ml (3 tbsp) lemon juice
75 g (3 oz) raisins
salt and pepper

1 Soak the almonds in boiling water for about 10 minutes. Drain and slice.

2 Heat the oil in a large wok or frying pan. Add the courgettes (in 2 batches if necessary) and the almonds. Stir-fry over a high heat for 7-8 minutes, adding a little more oil if necessary, until golden brown and just beginning to soften, but still crunchy.

3 Stir in the lemon juice, raisins and seasoning. Spoon into a bowl and serve cold, but not chilled.

Mixed Shredded Salad

Mix finely shredded lettuce (Cos or Webb), with shredded spring onions, beansprouts or red onion. Toss at the last minute with French Dressing (see page 18) and scatter over pink rose petals.

Summer Vegetable Platter

Either blanch, grill or barbecue a selection of summer vegetables, such as blanched asparagus spears, French beans, patty pan squashes, boiled new potatoes, sliced, oiled and grilled baby aubergines, red and yellow tomatoes and quartered and grilled peppers. Drizzle over a garlic dressing to serve. Garnish with sprigs of basil. For the dressing, skin and boil about 6 cloves garlic until very soft, drain. Blend with a little oil, vinegar and seasoning. Add a dash of cream before serving.

Easy Redcurrant Ice Cream

175 calories per serving

350 g (12 oz) fresh redcurrants
175 g (6 oz) granulated sugar
2 egg whites
300 ml (10 fl oz) double cream
frosted redcurrants, to decorate (see Cook's Tip)

1 Strip the redcurrants from their stalks and rinse. Purée in a food processor, then push through a nylon sieve to remove all the pips.

2 Dissolve the sugar in 125 ml (4 fl oz) water. Boil for about 5 minutes or until it becomes syrupy.

3 Whisk the egg whites until stiff, then gradually add the hot syrup, whisking all the time to keep the mixture stiff. Continue to whisk for about 5 minutes or until cool.

4 Whip the cream until it just holds its shape. Fold the cream and fruit purée through the egg white mixture and spoon into a freezer container. Freeze until firm — about 6 hours. Take out and leave at room temperature for 15 minutes to soften before serving.

COOK'S TIP

To frost redcurrants, brush the strips of berries with lightly whisked egg white and sprinkle with caster sugar. Place on foil and leave to dry at cool room temperature.

Easy Honey Ice Cream

190 calories per serving

60 ml (4 tbsp) runny honey
125 g (4 oz) granulated sugar
5 ml (1 tsp) ground cinnamon
300 ml (10 fl oz) thick pouring custard
2 egg whites
300 ml (10 fl oz) double cream

1 Place the honey, sugar and cinnamon in a saucepan with 125 ml (4 fl oz) water. Heat until the sugar dissolves, then boil for 5 minutes or until it becomes syrupy.

2 Complete and freeze the ice cream as above, folding the custard into the egg white mixture with the cream. Freeze overnight. Leave at cool room temperature for 10 minutes to soften before serving.

Redcurrants in Port

60 calories per serving

900 g (2 lb) redcurrants
50-125 g (2-4 oz) granulated sugar to taste
200 ml (7 fl oz) port
slices of Galia or Ogen melon, to accompany

1 Strip the redcurrants from their stalks using a fork, then rinse and drain.

2 Dissolve the sugar in the port with 150 ml (¼ pint) water. Boil for 2 minutes. Stir in the redcurrants and then immediately pour out into a heatproof bowl to cool.

3 Cover the redcurrants and chill before serving. Accompany with thick slices of either Galia or Ogen melon.

Easy Redcurrant Ice Cream,
Easy Honey Ice Cream, Redcurrants in Port

CELEBRATION BRUNCH

Make a special occasion out of an informal meal with this easy-to-prepare brunch.

Potato Pancakes topped with Smoked Salmon and Crème Fraîche or Garlic Mushrooms and Cheese

Grapefruit and Clementine Salad

Cinnamon Coffee Cake

Sparkling Cranberry Juice

Serves 8

Brunch is the perfect way to entertain informally and this menu can easily be supplemented with a bowl of fruit and a choice of soft cheeses to serve with bread. Sparkling cranberry juice, enhanced with sparkling wine or champagne, marks this as a special-occasion menu.

Countdown

THE DAY BEFORE
Make pancake batter to end of step 2; refrigerate. Prepare Grapefruit and Clementine Salad; refrigerate. Make Cinnamon Coffee Cake; store in an airtight container.

TO SERVE AT 11AM
9am Prepare pancakes to end of step 3.
10am Cook pancakes.
10.30am Reheat Cinnamon Coffee Cake, if wished. Prepare pancake toppings.
11am Serve brunch.

ALTERNATIVE CATERING QUANTITIES

(Standard recipes serve 8)

Guests	25	50	100
Potato Pancakes	x 3	x 6	x 12
Smoked Salmon and			
Crème Fraîche	x 3	x 6	x 12
Garlic Mushrooms and Cheese	x 3	x 6	x 12
Grapefruit and Clementine Salad	x 3	x 6	x 10
Greek natural yogurt	900 g	1.8 kg	2.7 kg
	(2 lb)	(4 lb)	(6 lb)
Cinnamon Coffee Cake	x 3	x 5	x 10

VITAL STATISTICS

Potato Pancakes
For larger numbers it is easiest to freeze them ahead. Thaw as directed. Place on baking sheets lined with non-stick paper. Cover with foil and reheat at 180°C (350°F) mark 4 for 15-20 minutes. Stack two layers of pancakes with non-stick paper between but no more or they won't heat properly. Alternatively, let each guest cook their own pancake but this can be messy!

Cinnamon Coffee Cake
This is at its best when served just warm. Cook ahead, freeze and reheat as directed.

FREEZER NOTES

Freeze pancakes between layers of greaseproof paper. Overwrap with foil; freeze. Thaw overnight at cool room temperature. Reheat in a moderate oven. Pack and freeze Cinnamon Coffee Cake. Thaw at cool room temperature for about 4 hours if wished. Reheat, wrapped in foil, at 180°C (350°F) mark 4 for 30 minutes.

Potato Pancakes

120 calories per pancake Makes about 16

700 g (1½ lb) potatoes, peeled
salt and pepper
75 ml (3 fl oz) milk
4 whole eggs, 5 egg whites
90 ml (6 tbsp) single cream
75 ml (5 tbsp) plain white flour
oil

1 Cook the potatoes in a pan of boiling, salted water for about 20 minutes or until cooked. Drain and mash well. Beat the milk, whole eggs, single cream and flour into the potatoes; season well.

2 Lightly whisk the egg whites and fold into the potato mixture. Cover and leave in a cool place for about 1 hour.

3 Heat a little oil in a non-stick crêpe pan and spoon in about 75 ml (5 tbsp) pancake mixture. Cook for about 2-3 minutes, then carefully flip over and cook the underside for a further 2-3 minutes. Cook the remaining pancakes.

4 Keep the pancakes hot in a low oven, layered with greaseproof paper and wrapped in foil. Serve them immediately with one of the following toppings.

Potato Pancakes

Smoked Salmon and Crème Fraîche

Tops about 8 pancakes

275 g (10 oz) sliced smoked salmon
200 ml (7 fl oz) crème fraîche or soured cream
40 g (1½ oz) jar salmon roe
fresh chives and lemon wedges, to garnish

1 Top each pancake with a slice of smoked salmon, a spoonful of crème fraîche and a little salmon roe.

2 Garnish the topped potato pancakes with fresh chives and lemon wedges.

Garlic Mushrooms and Cheese

Tops about 8 pancakes

75 g (3 oz) butter
1 clove garlic, skinned and crushed
ground turmeric
450 g (1 lb) assorted small mushrooms, such as: field, brown cap
175 g (6 oz) Esrom or Edam cheese, grated or pared

1 Melt the butter with the garlic and a little turmeric. Add the mushrooms and sauté for 2-3 minutes.

2 Spoon a little mixture over each pancake and top with some of the cheese.

Grapefruit and Clementine Salad

35 calories per serving

4 grapefruit
6 clementines
60 ml (4 tbsp) runny honey
juice of 1 lime
1 cm (½ in) piece fresh ginger, grated
Greek natural yogurt, to serve

1 Peel and slice the grapefruit and clementines; place in a non-metallic dish.

2 Whisk the runny honey, lime juice and fresh ginger together. Pour over the fruit, cover and leave to marinate for 8 hours. Serve with Greek natural yogurt.

Cinnamon Coffee Cake

420 calories per slice Makes 8 slices

125 g (4 oz) butter
200 g (7 oz) granulated sugar
2 eggs
150 g (5 oz) natural yogurt
10 ml (2 tsp) vanilla essence
125 g (4 oz) plain white flour
10 ml (2 tsp) baking powder
pinch of salt
150 g (5 oz) walnuts or pecan nuts, chopped
10 ml (2 tsp) ground cinnamon

1 Grease and base-line a 20.5 cm (8 in) deep round cake tin. Lightly dust with flour.

2 Cream together the butter with 175 g (6 oz) of the sugar. Beat in the eggs, yogurt and vanilla essence. Fold in the flour, baking powder and salt. Do not overbeat.

3 Mix together the remaining sugar, the walnuts or pecan nuts and cinnamon.

4 Spoon half the cake mixture into the prepared tin. Sprinkle over half the nut mixture. Add the remaining cake mix and top with the rest of the nuts and sugar.

5 Bake at 180°C (350°F) mark 4 for about 50 minutes, or until firm to the touch. Leave to cool in the tin for 20 minutes before turning out. Serve warm or cold with coffee.

Cinnamon Coffee Cake

Sparkling Cranberry Juice

Pour equal quantities of cranberry juice and sweet sparkling wine or champagne into glasses. (Cranberry juice is quite sharp, so you will need a slightly sweeter wine to counteract it.)

CHRISTENING LUNCH

A special-occasion menu to welcome a new arrival or to celebrate a wedding anniversary or birthday.

Smoked Salmon Savouries

Thai-style Lamb with Ginger

Lemon Sesame Potatoes

Shredded Red Salad

Strawberry Meringues

Celebration Cake

Serves 8

Organizing a celebration at home, whether it be a christening, birthday or wedding anniversary, needn't mean spending hours in the kitchen, not having time to see either your guests — or the new baby!

The Thai-style Lamb with Ginger can be prepared well in advance, and the Lemon Sesame Potatoes take just minutes to prepare, so both can look after themselves in the oven while everyone is enjoying the delicious Smoked Salmon Savouries with a glass of champagne. The Strawberry Meringues can also be made ahead of the day and stored in an airtight container. If you use a mixture of half caster sugar, half icing sugar, it produces a light, crisp meringue. These can be filled and decorated a couple of hours before you want to serve them.

The pretty Celebration Cake needn't take hours of icing and decorating. Keep it simple by adding a few fresh flowers and a silky ribbon.

Countdown

UP TO ONE MONTH BEFORE
Bake meringues and store them in an airtight container.

THE DAY BEFORE
Make Smoked Salmon Savouries to end of step 4. Cover loosely and refrigerate. Cook Thai-style Lamb with Ginger to end of step 4. Cool quickly, cover and refrigerate. Wash potatoes, boil for 5 minutes. Drain, cover and keep cool. Slice onions and thinly shred radicchio. Store in refrigerator in separate polythene bags. Make salad dressing, cover and refrigerate. Bake Celebration Cake. Fill and cover with icing and cut out name, but do not add ribbon or flowers yet.

TO SERVE AT 1PM
11am Assemble salad in bowl, but don't add dressing. Cover and refrigerate. Fill meringues and decorate with fruit. Cover loosely and refrigerate. Decorate cake with ribbon and flowers.

NOON Preheat oven to 200°C (400°F) mark 6.

12.05pm Bake Smoked Salmon Savouries. Serve warm.

12.15pm Stir cucumber and spring onion into lamb. Bring to boil, then cover and reheat in oven for about 40 minutes. Put potatoes in oven to bake.

12.45pm Toss salad with dressing.

12.50pm Dust meringues lightly with icing sugar.

1pm Serve Thai-style Lamb and accompaniments.

ALTERNATIVE CATERING QUANTITIES

(Standard recipes serves 8)

Guests	25	50	100
Smoked Salmon Savouries	x 2	x 3	x 5
Thai-style Lamb with Ginger	x 3	x 6	x 11
Lemon Sesame Potatoes	x 3	x 5	x 9
Shredded Red Salad	x 3	x 6	x 10
Dressing	x 2	x 5	x 8
Strawberry Meringues	x 3	x 5	x 9
Celebration Cake	x 2	x 3	x 5

VITAL STATISTICS
You will need plenty of oven space when preparing this menu.

Smoked Salmon Savouries
These are best served when they still retain a hint of warmth. Bake them just before the lamb is going into the oven.

Thai-style Lamb with Ginger
Lemon grass adds a wonderful fragrance to this recipe. It can be bought dried and preserved in jars but nothing beats the flavour of fresh lemon grass. After boning the lamb you should have about 1.1-1.4 kg (2¼-3 lb) meat.

Dressing for salad
As the quantities of salad increase you don't necessarily need to bulk up the dressing accordingly. Follow directions in chart.

Celebration Cake
Add lettering to the cake to suit the occasion. Or use the Chocolate and Orange Cake on page 137.

FREEZER NOTES
Freeze Smoked Salmon Savouries before glazing and baking. Glaze and cook from frozen at 200°C (400°F) mark 6 for 15 minutes. Wrap and freeze Celebration Cake at end of step 4. Thaw, wrapped at cool room temperature for about 6 hours. Fill and ice as directed. Don't freeze lamb, potato dish, salad or meringues.

Strawberry Meringues (page 42)

Smoked Salmon Savouries

20 calories per savoury Makes about 100 savouries

125 g (4 oz) butter, softened
225 g (8 oz) low-fat soft cheese
125 g (4 oz) plain white flour
50 g (2 oz) smoked salmon pieces
5 ml (1 tsp) chopped fresh dill
freshly ground black pepper
1 egg, beaten

1 Place the butter, 125 g (4 oz) of the soft cheese and the flour in a food processor and blend until the mixture forms a dough. Alternatively, beat the ingredients together using a wooden spoon, then knead the mixture lightly together. Wrap and chill for about 30 minutes.

2 Snip the salmon into small pieces and mix with the remaining cheese, the dill and pepper.

3 On a lightly floured surface, thinly roll out the dough. Cut into 4 cm (1½ in) wide strips. Cover half of the strips loosely with absorbent kitchen paper.

4 Place 1.25 ml (¼ tsp) of the salmon mixture at intervals down the strips. Brush around the edges and between the filling with beaten egg. Use the remaining pastry strips to cover the filling. Press in between the filling with the side of the hand to seal. Neaten the edges with a sharp knife, then cut at an angle to form diamonds. Brush evenly with the remaining egg.

5 Place the diamonds on a baking sheet. Bake at 200°C (400°F) mark 6 for 10 minutes until crisp and golden. Cool on a wire rack. Serve warm.

VARIATIONS

● Omit the smoked salmon and use 350 g (12 oz) full-fat soft cheese with herbs. Add more fresh herbs as wished.

● Omit the salmon and use 125 g (4 oz) chopped, peeled prawns.

● Use a creamy goat's cheese for the filling with 15 ml (1 tbsp) finely chopped spring onions. Top with a few poppy seeds at the end of step 4.

Thai – style Lamb with Ginger

460 calories per serving

2 kg (4½ lb) leg of lamb, boned
1 bunch spring onions, trimmed
oil
1 cucumber, thinly sliced
450 g (1 lb) onions, skinned and sliced
450 g (1 lb) baby turnips, thinly sliced
40 g (1½ oz) piece fresh root ginger, peeled and finely chopped
2 stalks lemon grass, or grated rind of 2 lemons
30 ml (2 tbsp) plain white flour
1.1 litres (2 pints) light stock
1 clove garlic, skinned and crushed
grated rind and juice of 2 oranges
salt and pepper
watercress, to garnish

1 Trim the lamb and cut into thin pieces. Cut the spring onions into thin finger-length shreds.

2 Heat 60 ml (4 tbsp) oil in a large flameproof casserole and brown the meat in batches, then remove with a slotted spoon and drain on absorbent kitchen paper. Sauté the cucumber and spring onions for 1 minute only. Remove and reserve.

3 Lower the heat and add the onions and turnips. Cook, stirring, until beginning to brown, adding a little more oil if necessary. Stir in the ginger, lemon grass (or lemon rind) and flour and cook for 1-2 minutes. Pour in the stock, garlic, grated orange rind and about 75 ml (5 tbsp) orange juice.

4 Replace the meat, season and bring to the boil. Cover tightly and cook at 170°C (325°F) mark 3 for 1 hour.

5 Stir in the reserved cucumber and spring onions and continue to cook for a further 30 minutes or until the lamb is very tender. Serve the lamb on a large heated platter, garnished with sprigs of fresh watercress.

COOK'S TIP

Lemon grass is available from Asian stores and many large supermarkets. It is a pale lemony colour and looks like a firm spring onion.

Lemon Sesame Potatoes

270 calories per serving

1.4 kg (3 lb) small new potatoes
salt
60 ml (4 tbsp) soy sauce
60 ml (4 tbsp) oil
60 ml (4 tbsp) lemon juice
25 g (1 oz) sesame seeds

1 Wash the potatoes well but don't peel. Halve any large ones. Cook in boiling salted water for 5 minutes only. Drain.

2 Place on one or two shallow roasting tins. Drizzle over the soy sauce, oil and lemon juice. Sprinkle over the sesame seeds.

3 Bake the potatoes in the oven at 200°C (400°F) mark 6 for about 45 minutes.

COOK'S TIP

If you are cooking the lamb and the potatoes together, set the oven at 200°C (400°F) mark 6 and cook the lamb for about 1 hour only — 45 minutes initially and then 15 minutes with the cucumber, etc.

Shredded Red Salad

90 calories per serving

225 g (8 oz) red onion, skinned and thinly sliced
2 small heads radicchio, thinly shredded
50 g (2 oz) beansprouts
30 ml (2 tbsp) sunflower oil
60 ml (4 tbsp) walnut oil
60 ml (4 tbsp) red wine
30 ml (2 tbsp) red wine vinegar
salt and pepper

1 Mix the red onion slices and shredded radicchio with the beansprouts.

2 Whisk together the oils, wine, vinegar and seasoning. Toss into the salad just before serving.

Strawberry Meringues

150 calories per meringue Makes about 12 meringues

3 egg whites
175 g (6 oz) caster sugar or 75 g (3 oz) caster sugar and 75 g (3 oz) sifted icing sugar
rosewater
300 ml (10 fl oz) double cream
icing sugar, strawberries, raspberries and rose leaves, to decorate

1 Cover two flat upturned baking sheets with pieces of non-stick baking parchment.

2 Place the egg whites in a large bowl and whisk steadily for about 1 minute or until a loose white foam forms. Add 5 ml (1 tsp) caster sugar and continue whisking until doubled in bulk.

3 Gradually whisk in the 75 g (3 oz) caster sugar, adding about 25 g (1 oz) at a time until the mixture is stiff and shiny. Continue whisking the mixture for about a further 5 minutes.

4 Sprinkle the remaining caster sugar (or the icing sugar) and a few drops of rosewater over the meringue mixture and fold in quickly but gently with a large metal spoon.

5 Shape the mixture into ovals with two teaspoons. Drop the mixture onto the prepared baking sheets, allowing room for the mixture to spread.

6 Cook in the oven at 110°C (225°F) mark ¼ for about 2 hours until completely dried out. (Swap the sheets around after 1 hour to ensure even drying.) Lift the meringues off the baking sheets and cool on wire racks.

7 Whip the cream until it just holds a soft peak and use to sandwich the meringues together. Pile on to a plate, dust with icing sugar and decorate with fresh strawberries and raspberries and rose leaves. Serve immediately or refrigerate for up to 2 hours before serving.

Celebration Cake

440 calories per slice Makes 16 slices

225 g (8 oz) butter or margarine
225 g (8 oz) caster sugar
4 eggs, beaten
225 g (8 oz) self-raising white flour
grated rind and juice of 1 lemon
red food colouring paste, or blue, or yellow
450 g (1 lb) ready-to-roll icing
300 ml (10 fl oz) double cream
120 ml (8 tbsp) black cherry conserve or 50 g (2 oz) sliced fruits such as strawberries
icing sugar
ribbon and fresh flowers, to decorate

1 Grease and base line a 23 cm (9 in) round cake tin, then set aside

2 Cream together the butter with the sugar until pale and fluffy. Add the eggs a little at a time, beating the mixture well after each addition.

3 Fold the flour into the mixture with the grated lemon rind and juice, using a large metal spoon.

4 Spoon into the tin and level the surface. Bake at 180°C (350°F) mark 4 for about 1-1¼ hours or until golden and firm to the touch. Cover the top with greaseproof paper, if necessary, towards the end of the cooking time. Turn out onto a wire rack to cool.

5 Meanwhile, colour the ready-to-roll icing. Dip a cocktail stick into the red paste and add a little to the icing. Thoroughly knead in the colour by repeatedly kneading and mixing the icing between finger and thumbs. Repeat, adding a little colour as necessary, until a pale pink colour is obtained. Wrap tightly.

6 Split the cake in half horizontally. Whip the cream until it just holds its shape, then fill the cake with jam or fruit and all but 45 ml (3 tbsp) cream. Place on a serving plate.

7 Spread the reserved cream thinly around the sides and over the top of the cake. Dust the work surface lightly with icing sugar and roll out the icing large enough to completely cover the cake. Fold the icing over a rolling pin and carefully lift it onto the cake, gently smooth the sides. Trim the extra icing from the base of the cake.

8 If wished, knead the icing trimmings together until smooth, then colour with a little more red paste to give a deeper pink. Roll out as before and carefully cut out the name or greeting, using letter cutters or cutting round cardboard templates.

9 Decorate with a broad ribbon and fresh flowers just before serving the cake.

Smoked Salmon Savouries (page 41)

FRIDAY NIGHT SUPPER

A delicious and informal meal to welcome your weekend guests.

Smoked Fish Gratin

Mixed Red Salad

Creamy Green Beans

Mustard Lemon Bread

Sticky Almond Cake

Orange Poached Fruits

Serves 8

Friday night is the beginning of the weekend. What better way to wind down from a busy week than to relax with friends or weekend guests and enjoy an informal meal together. Almost all of this tempting menu can be prepared in advance so you really can enjoy the evening.

The preparation for the Smoked Fish Gratin, Creamy Green Beans and Mustard Lemon Bread can be done the day before. Simply cook them when required. The almond cake is best made a week ahead, and the poached fruits can be prepared in advance.

Countdown

ABOUT A WEEK AHEAD
Make Sticky Almond Cake. Cool, wrap and store it in an air-tight tin.

THE DAY BEFORE
Complete Smoked Fish Gratin to end of step 4. Cool, cover and refrigerate leek and fish mixture. Cool and refrigerate pasta. Push a piece of damp greaseproof paper on to surface of sauce and refrigerate. If serving Creamy Green Beans cold, cook beans, make dressing and refrigerate them separately in polythene bags. Prepare mixed red salad ingredients and refrigerate them in a polythene bag. Don't slice radishes yet. Make French Dressing, cover and refrigerate until needed. Complete Mustard Lemon Bread to end of step 2. Refrigerate. Complete Orange Poached Fruits to end of step 2.

ON THE DAY—TO SERVE AT 8PM
6pm Remove Orange Poached Fruits from refrigerator. Add strawberries.

7pm Preheat oven to 200°C (400°F) mark 6. Complete Smoked Fish Gratin. (Warm cheese sauce gently before adding whisked egg whites.)

7.15pm Place Smoked Fish Gratin in oven to cook.

7.45pm Cook Creamy Green Beans, if serving hot. Toss hot or cold beans in prepared dressing. Toss salad. Heat Mustard Lemon Bread in the oven.

8pm Serve the meal.

FREEZER NOTES

Freeze Mustard Lemon Bread at end of step 2. Thaw overnight at cool room temperature, then complete as above. Wrap and freeze cooled Sticky Almond Cake. Thaw overnight at cool room temperature. Before serving, wrap cake in foil and warm in a hot oven for 10–12 minutes.

ALTERNATIVE CATERING QUANTITIES

(Standard recipes serve 8)

Guests	25	50	100
Smoked Fish Gratin	x 3	x 6	x 12
Mixed Red Salad	x 3	x 5	x 9
Creamy Green Beans	x 3	x 6	x 10
Mustard Lemon Bread	x 3	x 6	x 10
Pecan and Apple Meringue Cake	x 3	x 6	x 10
Sticky Almond Cake	x 3	x 6	x 10
Orange Poached Fruits	x 3	x 6	x 10

VITAL STATISTICS

You will need plenty of oven space here.

Smoked Fish Gratin
Use several medium sized dishes rather than one huge one as the gratin will heat through more evenly.

Creamy Green Beans
For large quantities it is much easier to serve the beans cold (see recipe).

Smoked Fish Gratin

Smoked Fish Gratin

530 calories per serving

900 g (2 lb) smoked haddock fillet

750 ml (1¼ pints) milk

butter

900 g (2 lb) leeks, trimmed and sliced

salt and pepper

150 ml (5 fl oz) double cream

225 g (8 oz) cooked, peeled prawns

125 g (4 oz) small pasta shapes, such as penne, farfalle

10 ml (2 tsp) oil

50 g (2 oz) plain white flour

125 g (4 oz) Cheddar cheese, grated

15 ml (1 tbsp) Dijon mustard

30 ml (2 tbsp) chopped fresh parsley

2 egg whites

flat-leaf parsley sprigs and king prawns, to garnish

Mixed Red Salad, to serve

1 Place the fish in a roasting tin or large frying pan. Pour over about 600 ml (1 pint) of the milk. Slowly bring to the boil, cover and simmer gently for 10-12 minutes or until tender. Remove the fish from the milk and cool slightly. Strain the milk into a jug; reserve. Flake the fish into a bowl, discarding skin and bones.

2 Melt 50 g (2 oz) butter in a pan and cook the leeks for 10 minutes or until very soft but not brown. Season. Stir in the cream then add to the haddock with the prawns.

3 Cook the pasta in boiling, salted water for about 8 minutes or until just tender. Drain, then stir in the oil.

4 Rinse out the pasta pan, then melt 50 g (2 oz) butter. Off the heat, stir in the flour and gradually add the reserved milk and remaining milk. Bring to the boil, stirring, and boil for 2 minutes. Remove from the heat and stir in 50 g (2 oz) of the cheese, the mustard and parsley.

5 Mix the pasta with the leek and fish mixture and place in one 3.4 litre (6 pint) or two 2 litre (3½ pint) ovenproof dishes. Whisk the egg whites until they stand in stiff peaks. Gently fold into the cheese sauce, then pour over the leek and pasta mixture. Sprinkle with the remaining cheese.

6 Cook at 200°C (400°F) mark 6 for about 40-45 minutes or until golden brown. Garnish with flat-leaf parsley and prawns and serve with the Mixed Red Salad.

Mixed Red Salad

73 calories per serving

1 head raddichio

1 head red chicory

1 small red onion, skinned and sliced

125 g (4 oz) cherry tomatoes, halved

75 ml (5 tbsp) French Dressing (see page 18)

few radishes (optional)

spring onion tops, to garnish (optional)

1 Rinse, drain and dry the raddichio and chicory leaves. Shred or tear into smaller pieces.

2 Just before serving, toss the raddichio, chicory, onion and tomatoes in the French Dressing. Add a few sliced radishes and garnish with spring onion tops, if wished.

Creamy Green Beans

60 calories per serving

700 g (1½ lb) fine green beans

salt and pepper

30 ml (2 tbsp) mayonnaise

30 ml (2 tbsp) natural yogurt

15 ml (1 tbsp) wholegrain mustard

1 Cook the beans in a pan of boiling, salted water for about 4 minutes. Drain well.

2 Mix together the mayonnaise, yogurt, mustard and seasoning, then stir into the hot beans. Alternatively, serve the beans cold as a salad.

Mustard Lemon Bread

180 calories per serving

75-125 g (3-4 oz) butter, softened

15 ml (1 tbsp) wholegrain mustard

grated rind and juice of 1 lemon

1 French loaf

1 Beat together the butter and mustard with the grated lemon rind and 5 ml (1 tsp) lemon juice.

2 Slice the bread, but do not cut all the way through. Butter the slices and over the top. Wrap loosely in foil and heat at 200°C (400°F) mark 6 for 15 minutes.

Sticky Almond Cake

480 calories per serving

225 g (8 oz) butter

225 g (8 oz) caster sugar

4 eggs, beaten

50 g (2 oz) white plain flour

175 g (6 oz) ground almonds

2.5 ml (½ tsp) almond essence

350 g (12 oz) white marzipan

icing sugar, to dust

1 Grease and base-line a 21.5-23 cm (8½-9 inch) base-measurement, spring-release cake tin.

2 Cream together the butter and sugar until very pale. Gradually beat in the eggs, adding a little flour if the mixture curdles.

3 Roll out the marzipan slightly larger than the cake tin. Using the tin as a template, cut the marzipan into a circle.

4 Place half the cake mixture in the cake tin. Top with the marzipan, then finish with the cake mixture.

5 Bake at 180°C (350°F) mark 4 for about 1¼ hours or until firm to the touch, covering lightly with foil if necessary. Cool for 5 minutes in the tin, then remove from the tin and cool on a wire rack. Wrap in foil and store for at least 1 day before serving. Dust with icing sugar.

Orange Poached Fruits

55 calories per serving

6 ripe peaches or nectarines

450 ml (15 fl oz) orange juice

15 ml (1 tbsp) caster sugar

pinch ground cinnamon

350 g (12oz) strawberries

strips of orange rind, to decorate (optional)

1 Halve, quarter and stone the peaches. Place in a saucepan with the orange juice, sugar and cinnamon. Simmer gently for 5 minutes. Remove from the heat and place the drained peaches in a bowl.

2 Bubble down the juice until reduced by about half. Pour over the fruit. Cool, cover and refrigerate.

3 Hull and halve the strawberries. Take the fruit out of the refrigerator about 2 hours before serving; add the strawberries. Decorate if wished.

SATURDAY LUNCH

An informal help-yourself buffet lunch for a busy day.

Roasted Vegetable Soup
with Olive and Basil Cream

Picnic Platter

Hazelnut and Chocolate Flapjacks

Serves 8

With people coming and going over the weekend, especially around lunchtime, it's best to keep the menu flexible. Prepare simple, light food that isn't going to spoil when everyone's on the go. Leave the table set and the soup ready, and allow your guests to help themselves, buffet style.

Roasted Vegetable Soup, topped with Olive and Basil Cream, can be prepared up to two days before or frozen ahead.

A colourful selection of cheeses, fruit, salamis, olives and bread provides a wealth of choice in the Picnic Platter — careful shopping is all that is required for this. The scrumptious Flapjacks round off the lunch and these can also be baked in advance.

So when time is precious on a Saturday, cooks can also have some time to themselves or simply relax if sharing lunch with family or friends.

Countdown

UP TO A WEEK BEFORE
Make Flapjacks.

UP TO 2 DAYS BEFORE
Prepare soup and Olive and Basil Cream. Cover and chill.

ON THE MORNING
Assemble the platter.

FREEZER NOTES

Pack and freeze soup at the end of step 3. Thaw overnight at cool room temperature; chill again before serving. Pack and freeze Flapjacks. Thaw for 4 hours.

VITAL STATISTICS

Bread

Loaves vary greatly in size. One medium sized loaf (uncut) will serve about five to six people. The quantities above are based on this.

ALTERNATIVE CATERING QUANTITIES

(Standard recipes serve 8)

Guests	25	50	100
Roasted Vegetable Soup	x 3	x 6	x 10
Olive and Basil Cream	x 3	x 6	x 10
Picnic Platter			
Salamis	2.3 kg	4 kg	7.2 kg
	(5 lb)	(9 lb)	(16 lb)
Cheeses	1.8 kg	3,2 kg	5.4 kg
	(4 lb)	(7 lb)	(12 lb)
Olives	700 g	1.1 kg	1.8 kg
	(1½ lb)	(2½ lb)	(4 lb)
Fruit	2.7 kg	5 kg	9 kg
	(6 lb)	(11 lb)	(20 lb)
Bread	5 loaves	9 loaves	16 loaves
Hazelnut and			
Chocolate Flapjacks	x 2	x 4	x 7

Roasted Vegetable Soup with Olive and Basil Cream

165 calories per serving

1.4 kg (3 lb) ripe tomatoes, halved
350 g (12 oz) shallots or onion, skinned and halved
275 g (10 oz) celery, chopped
4 small cloves garlic, skinned
275 g (10 oz) carrots, sliced
4 red peppers, chopped
60 ml (4 tbsp) olive oil
2 red chillies
750 ml (1¼ pints) passata (see Cook's Tip)
7.5 ml (1½ tsp) sugar
grated rind and juice of 1 lime
salt and pepper
crushed ice, to serve
Olive and Basil Cream, to accompany

1 Divide all the vegetables between two roasting tins. Add the oil and chillies, then stir well. Roast at 200°C (400°F) mark 6 for 1-1½ hours or until the skins are charred, turning halfway through the cooking time.

2 Discard the chillies. Blend the vegetables with the passata, then push the purée through a sieve.

3 Add the sugar, grated lime rind and 30 ml (2 tbsp) juice and plenty of seasoning. Cover and chill.

4 Serve the soup sprinkled with crushed ice and top with Olive and Basil Cream.

COOK'S TIP
Passata, a mixture of sieved tomatoes rather like tomato paste, is sold in cartons and bottles. Look out for it in supermarkets.

Olive and Basil Cream

75 calories per serving

50 g (2 oz) pitted black olives
150 ml (5 fl oz) crème fraîche
30 ml (2 tbsp) chopped fresh basil
grated rind and juice of 1 lemon
salt and pepper

1 Roughly chop the olives. Stir into the crème fraîche with the basil, grated lemon rind and about 10 ml (2 tsp) juice. Season well.

2 Cover and chill the cream until ready to serve, then spoon on to the soup.

Picnic Platter

Buy a selection of different breads and arrange platters of salamis and olives, cheeses and fruit. As well as farmhouse Cheddar, you could include creamy French Vignotte, fresh goat's cheese and Mozzarella.

Hazelnut and Chocolate Flapjacks

215 calories per serving Makes about 12

125 g (4 oz) soft light brown sugar
125 g (4 oz) butter or margarine
15 ml (1 tbsp) golden syrup
50 g (2 oz) hazelnuts, roughly chopped
175 g (6 oz) jumbo or porridge oats
50 g (2 oz) milk chocolate drops

1 Lightly grease a shallow, oblong baking tin measuring 28 x 18 cm (11 x 7 in).

2 Melt together the sugar, butter and syrup. Stir in the hazelnuts and oats. Allow to cool slightly, then stir in the chocolate drops.

3 Spoon the mixture into the tin. Bake at 180°C (350°F) mark 4 for about 25 minutes or until golden and firm.

4 Cool in the tin for a few minutes before cutting into squares. Turn out onto a wire rack to cool completely. Store in an airtight container for up to a week.

Roasted Vegetable Soup

SATURDAY EVENING SUPPER

Turn Saturday into a special occasion with this irresistible menu that makes the most of fresh produce.

Spinach, Bacon and Roquefort Salad

Spiced Pork Sauté

Curried Cashew Nuts

Vegetable Couscous

Iced Lime Mousse

Summer Berries

Serves 8

The highlight of the weekend, this menu, with three mouth-watering courses all full of colour, will provide a Saturday evening supper to remember.

The oven toasted French bread, pine nuts and bacon mixed with spinach and Roquefort make a marvellous warm salad starter. The pork sauté with fresh pineapple is served with flavoured cashew nuts and a vegetable couscous tossed in a mustard and honey dressing. The tangy dessert to round off the supper is a lime mousse with mixed summer berries.

Countdown

ONE WEEK BEFORE
Prepare Curried Cashew Nuts

UP TO 2 DAYS BEFORE
Make Iced Lime Mousse

THE DAY BEFORE
Follow step 1 and 2 of Spinach, Bacon and Roquefort Salad. Store cold croûtes and remaining ingredients in separate containers in refrigerator. Follow steps 1, 2 and 3 of Spiced Pork Sauté, but do not brown meat; cover and refrigerate. Use about 30 ml (2 tbsp) oil to brown onions, etc in step 2. Cool, cover and refrigerate sauce at end of step 3. Prepare Summer Berries to end of step 2.

THE MORNING
Prepare broccoli, mangetout and fennel and refrigerate in polythene bags. Make couscous dressing, but don't add spring onions and chives. Refrigerate in a polythene bag.

TO SERVE AT 8PM
6pm Take salad out of refrigerator.
7.30pm Brown pork, set aside.
7.45pm Bring pork and sauce to boil. Add pineapple. Simmer for 10 minutes and garnish to serve.
7.55pm Pour water over couscous.
8pm Take Summer Berries out of refrigerator. Toss the salad ingredients together and serve meal. Between starter and main course, blanch vegetables for couscous and complete.

ALTERNATIVE CATERING QUANTITIES

(Standard recipes serve 8)

Guests	25	50	100
Spinach, Bacon and Roquefort Salad	x 3	x 6	x 10
Spiced Pork Sauté	x 3	x 6	x 10
Curried Cashew Nuts	x 2	x 4	x 6
Vegetable Couscous	x 3	x 6	x 10
Iced Lime Mousse	x 2	x 4	x 8
Summer Berries	x 3	x 6	x 10

VITAL STATISTICS

Spiced Pork Sauté
When cooking for large numbers it is unlikely that you will want to brown all the meat at the last minute. For ease, follow the recipe but add the meat in step 3 allowing it to cook uncovered for 15-20 minutes. Cool, cover and refrigerate for up to a day. Bring slowly to the boil and simmer for 5-10 minutes to heat thoroughly, stirring occasionally. Add the pineapple and complete as in basic recipe. Do not cook more than double quantity at one time or the sauce will not reduce sufficiently. Use 450 ml (¾ pint) white wine only and 750 ml (1¼ pints) stock only for double quantity of recipe. It's best to reheat it in manageable quantities too to ensure that it is piping hot.

Vegetable Couscous
For larger quantities blanch all the vegetables ahead of time, then cover and refrigerate. Remove from the refrigerator at least 2 hours before serving. Fold into the warm couscous with the dressing just before serving.

Iced Lime Mousse
If you have very large mixing bowls this can be made in double quantities.

Spinach, Bacon and Roquefort Salad

520 calories per serving

8 slices of French bread, cut on the diagonal, about 2.5 cm (1 in) thick
120 ml (8 tbsp) olive oil
175 g (6 oz) streaky bacon or pancetta (Italian bacon), sliced very thinly
50 g (2 oz) pinenuts
60 ml (4 tbsp) sesame oil
30 ml (2 tbsp) red wine vinegar
freshly ground black pepper
125 g (4 oz) Roquefort cheese, crumbled
175 g (6 oz) black seedless grapes, halved
125 g (4 oz) baby spinach, washed

1 Brush both sides of each slice of French bread with 60 ml (4 tbsp) of the olive oil. Place on a baking sheet. Halve or chop the bacon and place on a baking sheet with the pinenuts. Cook at 230°C (450°F) mark 8 for about 10 minutes or until golden brown, turning halfway.

2 Whisk the remaining 60 ml (4 tbsp) olive oil with the sesame oil, vinegar and pepper.

3 Toss all the salad ingredients and dressing together to serve.

Spiced Pork Sauté

345 calories per serving

900 g (2 lb) pork fillet
about 45 ml (3 tbsp) oil
225 g (8 oz) onions, skinned and roughly chopped
1 clove garlic, skinned and crushed
5 ml (1 tsp) sugar
1 small red chilli, seeded and chopped
15 ml (1 tbsp) ground coriander
2.5 ml (½ tsp) ground turmeric
5-10 ml (1-2 tsp) hot curry paste
450 ml (¾ pint) light stock
300 ml (½ pint) white wine
150 ml (5 fl oz) double cream
225 g (8 oz) fresh pineapple, thinly sliced (½ small pineapple)
salt and pepper
30 ml (2 tbsp) chopped fresh coriander
Curried Cashew Nuts and fresh coriander, to garnish

1 Slice the pork fillet into 1 cm (½in) pieces. Heat the oil in a large, shallow flameproof casserole and brown the meat in batches. Drain on absorbent kitchen paper.

2 Add the onions, garlic and sugar. Fry for about 5 minutes, adding a little more oil if necessary. Stir in the chilli, ground coriander and turmeric, then fry for a further 1 minute.

3 Stir in the curry paste, stock, wine and cream. Bring to the boil and simmer for 10-15 minutes or until well reduced.

4 Add the meat, pineapple and seasoning and simmer for a further 5 minutes or until the meat is tender.

5 Stir in the chopped coriander. Garnish with the nuts and coriander to serve.

Curried Cashew Nuts

110 calories per serving

15 ml (1 tbsp) oil
125 g (4 oz) unsalted cashew nuts
10 ml (2 tsp) medium curry powder
salt and pepper

1 Heat the oil in a non-stick frying pan and cook the nuts, curry powder and seasoning over a medium heat for 3-4 minutes or until lightly browned, stirring occasionally.

2 Cool the curried nuts completely. Roughly chop the nuts before serving.

Spinach, Bacon and Roquefort Salad

Vegetable Couscous

370 calories per serving

350 g (12 oz) couscous

225 g (8 oz) broccoli, cut into small florets

125 g (4 oz) mangetout, trimmed

225 g (8 oz) fennel, trimmed and sliced

salt and pepper

125 g (4 oz) petit pois

grated rind and juice of 2 lemons

175 ml (6 fl oz) olive oil

60 ml (4 tbsp) wholegrain mustard

30 ml (2 tbsp) runny honey

1 bunch spring onions, trimmed and chopped

1 bunch chives, snipped

1 Place the couscous in a bowl and pour over 600 ml (1 pint) boiling water. Cover with foil and leave to stand for about 10 minutes or until all the water is absorbed.

2 Blanch the broccoli, mangetout and fennel together in boiling, salted water with the petit pois for about 2 minutes.

3 Meanwhile, whisk together the grated rind of 1 lemon and 75 ml (5 tbsp) juice, the oil, wholegrain mustard, honey and seasoning. Stir the onions and chives into the dressing.

4 Drain the vegetables and fold into the warm couscous with the dressing. Serve immediately.

Iced Lime Mousse

520 calories per serving

125 g (4 oz) butter

5 eggs (see Note)

200 g (7 oz) caster sugar

grated rind and juice of 5-6 limes

450 ml (15 fl oz) double cream

Summer Berries, to serve

1 Place the butter in a bowl and melt over a pan of gently simmering water.

2 Using an electric whisk, beat the eggs and sugar until pale and mousse-like and doubled in volume. Add the butter. Continue whisking over a gentle heat until the mixture thickens and leaves a trail on itself for 2-3 seconds. (This will take about 20 minutes.)

3 Remove from the heat. Stir in the grated rind of the limes and 175 ml (6 fl oz) juice. Cool.

4 Whisk the cream until it just holds its shape, then fold into the lime mixture. Pour into a freezerproof serving dish and freeze for at least 6 hours, preferably overnight.

5 Allow the mousse to stand at room temperature for 5 minutes before serving with the berries. Spoon a few berries over the mousse, if wished.

NOTE

The young, the elderly, pregnant women and those suffering from immune deficiency diseases should not eat raw eggs.

Summer Berries

60 calories per serving

50 g (2 oz) sugar

225 g (8 oz) very ripe strawberries

900 g (2 lb) mixed strawberries, redcurrants, blackberries and raspberries, prepared

2-3 green cardamom pods, crushed

lime slices, to decorate

1 Blend the sugar and strawberries in a food processor. Push through a nylon sieve.

2 Stir the remaining fruit into the purée. Add the cardamom. Cover and chill. Serve the berries with the mousse decorated with lime slices.

Iced Lime Mousse with Summer Berries

SUNDAY LUNCH

A perfect end to the weekend, try this roast with a difference.

Peppered Beef with Anchovy and Herb Sauce

Crispy Potatoes with Rosemary

Mixed Beans and Baby Carrots

Cherry Brûlées

Serves 8

A succulent topside of beef coated and roasted in crushed peppercorns, then served with an anchovy, herb and shallot sauce will make this a Sunday lunch to remember. The meal ends with mouthwatering Cherry Brûlées - Kirsch-soaked cherries baked with a creamy egg custard, then coated in golden caramel.

Countdown

UP TO THREE DAYS BEFORE
Complete Cherry Brûlées to end of step 4. Chill.

TO SERVE AT 1PM
10.30am Finish brûlées and return to refrigerator. Soak anchovies and chop shallots for Anchovy and Herb Sauce. Set aside in a cool place.

11am Preheat oven to 200°C (400°F) mark 6. Prepare 1.4-1.6 kg (3-3½ lb) mixed beans and baby carrots.

11.30am Prepare beef and place in oven at about 11.30 am (depending on cooking times).

12.10pm Put Crispy Potatoes with Rosemary in to cook.

12.50pm Cook beans and carrots. Remove beef from oven. Transfer to a heatproof serving dish. Turn oven down to low and return beef, loosely covered. Make Anchovy and Herb Sauce.

VITAL STATISTICS

You will need plenty of oven space here.

Peppered Beef with Anchovy and Herb Sauce

When cooking in quantity, buy several 1.8 kg (4 lb) topside joints rather than one huge joint—it is easier to get an even cooking with a smaller piece of meat. Cook the joints in rotation so that they don't all come out of the oven at once. Prepare gravy ahead of time using a little olive oil in place of the meat juices. Reheat to serve adding the butter and herbs at the last minute. Recruit a good carver and use a very sharp knife.

Crispy Potatoes with Rosemary

Do not pile too many potatoes into one roasting tin or the centre potatoes will be soggy.

Mixed Beans and Baby Carrots

If possible blanch vegetables ahead of time ready to reheat in batches in the microwave. Or serve as a salad tossed with a little French Dressing.

Cherry Brûlées

Prepare quantities as above dividing the mixture between 25/50/100 ramekins. Prepare the custard in no more than double quantity at one time. The caramel sets quickly so it is best to prepare it in single batches only. Alternatively, pour each quantity of custard over the cherries in a 1.1 litre (2 pint) shallow ovenproof dish as in the basic recipe for about 45-60 minutes. Top with caramel and cherries.

ALTERNATIVE CATERING QUANTITIES

(Standard recipes serve 8)

Guests	25	50	100
Peppered Beef with Anchovy and Herb Sauce	x 3	x 6	x 10
Crispy Potatoes with Rosemary	x 2½	x 5	x 9
Green beans/carrots/ broad beans (total weight)	4 kg (9 lb)	7.2 kg (16 lb)	13.5 kg (30 lb)
Cherry Brûlées	x 3	x 6	x 12

Cherry Brûlée

Peppered Beef with Anchovy and Herb Sauce

575 calories per serving

75 g (3 oz) black peppercorns
1.8 kg (4 lb) rolled topside of beef
30 ml (2 tbsp) oil
salt
50 g (2 oz) can anchovy fillets, drained
50 ml (2 fl oz) milk
2 shallots, skinned and finely chopped
juice of 1 lemon
3 cloves garlic, skinned and crushed
30 ml (2 tbsp) Worcestershire sauce
300 ml (½ pint) beef stock
150 ml (¼ pint) brandy
75 g (3 oz) unsalted butter
60 ml (4 tbsp) chopped fresh parsley and thyme
mixed beans and baby carrots, to serve

1 Put the peppercorns in a pestle and mortar or a food processor; blend until coarsely ground. Brush the meat with 15 ml (1 tbsp) of the oil, season with salt, then roll in the peppercorns, coating completely.

2 Place the remaining 15 ml (1 tbsp) oil in a roasting tin with the meat. For rare beef, cook at 200°C (400°F) mark 6 for about 1 hour, basting frequently. (Cook beef for 15 minutes per 0.5 kg (1 lb) for rare, 20 minutes per 0.5 kg (1 lb) for medium rare and 25 minutes per 0.5 kg (1 lb) for well done.)

3 Meanwhile, soak the drained anchovies in the milk for at least 5-10 minutes. When the meat is cooked, keep warm, covered, in a serving dish in a low oven. Drain off the fat from the roasting tin but retain the beef juices. Add the shallots and stir over a low heat for 1-2 minutes or until just coloured. Drain the anchovies and add, stirring, until dissolved.

4 Add 30 ml (2 tbsp) lemon juice, garlic, Worcestershire sauce, stock and brandy. Bring to the boil and begin whisking in the butter, a little at a time, until smooth. Add the herbs. Serve immediately with mixed beans and carrots.

Crispy Potatoes with Rosemary

225 calories per serving

1.4 kg (3 lb) new potatoes
90 ml (6 tbsp) olive or vegetable oil
4 cloves garlic
1 rosemary sprig or 5 ml (1 tsp) dried
salt

1 Cook the potatoes in a pan of boiling water for 5 minutes, then drain.

2 Heat the oil in a roasting tin at 200°C (400°F) mark 6 for 2 minutes. Add the potatoes, whole garlic and rosemary. Cook for 35-40 minutes, turning the potatoes occasionally, until golden brown and crisp.

3 Drain the potatoes on absorbent kitchen paper and sprinkle with salt.

Cherry Brûlées

395 calories per serving

350 g (12 oz) fresh cherries
15 ml (1 tbsp) Kirsch
4 egg yolks
50 g (2 oz) caster sugar
450 ml (15 fl oz) double cream
125 g (4 oz) granulated sugar

1 Stone the cherries, reserving eight with stems for decoration. Pour the Kirsch over the remaining pitted cherries.

2 Whisk together the egg yolks and caster sugar until they have thickened and lightened in colour. Pour in the cream, stirring. Place in a heavy-based saucepan. Cook over a low heat, stirring continuously, until the mixture thickens to the consistency of double cream. This will take about 10 minutes. Do not boil.

3 Divide the soaked cherries among eight ramekins or heat-proof cups. Strain over the custard mixture. Place in a roasting tin with warm water to come half way up their sides. Cover the tin with foil.

4 Bake at 150°C (300°F) mark 2 for 30-35 minutes or until very lightly set. Cool and refrigerate until firm.

5 Place the granulated sugar in a small, heavy-based saucepan. Heat gently until the sugar dissolves and turns a golden caramel colour. Place a reserved cherry on each ramekin. Pour a thin layer of the caramel over each. Chill the brûlées, uncovered, for about 1 hour but no more than 6 hours before serving.

CHRISTMAS COCKTAIL PARTY

Cocktail parties are always popular at this time of year, so delight your guests with these tempting nibbles and be guaranteed a successful party.

Nutty Chicken Bites

Nan Bread with Spicy Prawns

Smoked Salmon Roulade

Quick Canapé ideas

Leek and Goat's Cheese Purses

Baked New Potatoes with
Soured Cream and Bacon

Walnut Biscuits with Stilton and Celery

Cheese Croustades with Aubergine

Mini Florentines

There is something for everyone in this irresistible selection of hot and cold canapés: choose from original, traditional, vegetarian and even sweet variations. Select a colourful range of tastes and textures, remembering that the greater the variety of canapés you serve the more you will have to make as inevitably we all like to have a taste of everything!

Countdown

TWO WEEKS BEFORE
Complete steps 1-3 of Cheese Croustades with Aubergine.

ONE WEEK BEFORE
Make Walnut Biscuits. Cool and store in airtight containers.

FOUR DAYS BEFORE
Make dip for Baked New Potatoes with Soured Cream and Bacon, cover and refrigerate.

THREE DAYS BEFORE
Make dip for Nutty Chicken Bites, cover and refrigerate. Make Florentines.

TWO DAYS BEFORE
Complete Smoked Salmon Roulade to end of step 3.

THE DAY BEFORE
Marinate chicken overnight for Nutty Chicken Bites. Cook potatoes for Baked New Potatoes.

ON THE DAY
IN THE MORNING
Complete step 1 of Nan Bread with Spicy Prawns. Cover ingredients and refrigerate. Make Leek and Goat's Cheese Purses to end of step 3; cover and refrigerate. Cook as directed. Make topping for Walnut Biscuits. Prepare Stilton mixture and aubergine topping for Cheese Croustades, cover and refrigerate.

TWO HOURS BEFORE
Complete Cheese Croustades with Aubergine.

ONE HOUR BEFORE
Top Walnut Biscuits.

30 MINUTES BEFORE
Reheat potatoes for Baked New Potatoes at 180°C (350°F) mark 4 for 20 minutes. Finish any remaining recipes.

CATERING QUANTITIES

For 25 people prepare about 300 canapés (12 each)
For 50 people prepare about 450 canapés (9 each)
For 100 people prepare about 600 canapés (6 each)

VITAL STATISTICS

Canapés are time-consuming to make and to finish off, so do allow plenty of time for this. Plenty of pairs of hands are a great help for the last minute cooking and garnishing.

FREEZER NOTES

Freeze Leek and Goat's Cheese Purses at end of step 3. Cook from frozen. Open-freeze uncooked Walnut Biscuits on baking sheets. Cook from frozen for 15-20 minutes. Pack and freeze bread bases of Cheese Croustades only. Thaw at cool room temperature for 1 hour. Complete as recipe. Cool cooked Mini Florentines, pack and freeze with or without chocolate. Thaw at cool room temperature for about 2 hours. Nutty Chicken Bites, Nan Bread with Spicy Prawns, Smoked Salmon Roulade, Baked New Potatoes with Soured Cream and Bacon and Quick Canapé Ideas will not freeze.

Canapés

Nutty Chicken Bites

20 calories per chicken bite 95 calories per 15 ml (1 tbsp) dip
Makes about 70 chicken bites

900 g (2 lb) skinless chicken breast fillets
125 g (4 oz) onion, skinned and finely chopped
90 ml (6 tbsp) dark soy sauce
50 ml (10 tsp) dark muscovado sugar
15 ml (1 tbsp) oil
2 cloves garlic, skinned and crushed
5 ml (1 tsp) mild curry powder
10-15 ml (2-3 tsp) mild chilli powder
450 g (1 lb) crunchy peanut butter
pinch of salt
½ medium cucumber

1 Bat out the chicken breasts between sheets of greaseproof paper. Cut into 2.5 cm (1 in) pieces.

2 Mix the onion with the soy sauce and 20 ml (4 tsp) of the sugar. Pour over the chicken and toss well. Cover and refrigerate overnight.

3 Meanwhile, make the dip. Heat the oil in a pan and cook the garlic, curry and chilli powders for 1-2 minutes. Add the peanut butter, salt and remaining sugar with 450 ml (¾ pint) water. Simmer for 5 minutes, stirring, until thick.

4 Thread the chicken onto cocktail sticks. Cook at 220°C (425°F) mark 7 for 10 minutes until cooked through. Cut the cucumber into 1 cm (½ in) pieces and thread onto the sticks. Serve with the cold dip.

Nan Bread with Spicy Prawns

25 calories per bread square Makes about 60

15 ml (1 tbsp) oil
1 clove garlic, skinned and crushed
10 ml (2 tsp) mild curry powder
4 spring onions, trimmed and finely chopped
350 g (12 oz) cooked, peeled prawns, roughly chopped
20 ml (4 tsp) mango chutney
20 ml (4 tsp) natural yogurt
salt and pepper
2 large nan bread, about 275 g (10 oz) total weight

1 Heat the oil in a frying pan and cook the garlic, curry powder and onions for 1 minute, stirring. Add the prawns. Cook gently for a further 2-3 minutes. Off the heat, stir in the chutney and yogurt. Season and set aside.

2 Heat the nan bread in the oven according to the packet instructions. Cut into small squares and top with a little of the prawn mixture. Serve warm or cold.

Smoked Salmon Roulade

20 calories per round Makes 70 rounds

1 large bunch watercress
225 g (8 oz) full-fat soft cheese with garlic and herbs
10 ml (2 tsp) lemon juice
freshly ground black pepper
225 g (8 oz) smoked salmon
lemon wedges, to garnish

1 Finely chop the watercress, discarding any coarse stalks. Using an electric whisk, mix into the soft cheese with the lemon juice and plenty of black pepper.

2 Cut out a piece of greaseproof paper 30.5 x 33 cm (12 x 13 in). Lay the pieces of smoked salmon on top, overlapping each piece slightly to form a rectangle about 30.5 x 28 cm (12 x 11 in). Cut in half widthways to make two rectangles.

3 Spread the soft cheese mixture over both rectangles, then carefully roll each one into a thin sausage, using the paper to help you. Cover and refrigerate overnight.

4 Cut each roll into 5 mm (¼ in) slices and serve immediately garnished with wedges of lemon.

Quick Canapé Ideas

● Thread half a cherry tomato onto a cocktail stick with a basil leaf and a wedge of feta cheese.

● Place 900 g (2 lb) cocktail sausage in a roasting tin. Add a 350 g (12 oz) jar of mango chutney, 15 ml (1 tbsp) wholegrain mustard and 10 ml (2 tsp) lemon juice. Stir until the sausages are fully coated. Cook at 190°C (375°F) mark 5 for 45-50 minutes or until cooked through and golden brown. Stir halfway through the cooking time. Serve warm.

● Roll out and cut 5 cm (2 in) squares from puff pastry. Fold two corners into the centre, press down and brush with beaten egg. Bake at 200°C (400°F) mark 6 for 8-10 minutes. Top with soft cheese and smoked salmon; sprinkle with lemon juice and black pepper.

● Top 1 cm (½ in) slices of cucumber with taramasalata. Garnish with a dill sprig.

● Spread slices of pumpernickel with mayonnaise mixed with chopped fresh dill. Top with slices of smoked salmon cut into squares. Or use gravadlax and the mustard sauce with which it is often sold.

Leek and Goat's Cheese Purses

35 calories per savoury Makes 48

butter
225 g (8 oz) leeks, cleaned and finely chopped
125 g (4 oz) crumbly goat's cheese such as Crottin de Chavignol, crumbled
50 g (2 oz) sun-dried tomatoes in oil, drained and chopped
salt and pepper
eight 31 x 45.5 cm (12¼x 18 in) sheets filo pastry

1 Heat 25 g (1 oz) butter in a frying pan and cook the leeks for 4-5 minutes until softened. Cool, then add the cheese and tomatoes. Season.

2 Place one sheet of filo on a work surface and brush with melted butter. Place another piece next to it, overlapping the long edges by about 2.5 cm (1 in). Brush lightly with melted butter. Place two more pieces on top in the same way, brushing lightly with butter. You should have a 59 x 45.5 cm (23½ x 18 in) oblong. Place 5 ml (1 tsp) mixture at 5 cm (2 in) intervals on the pastry.

3 Top with sheets of filo as before, buttering between the layers. Press the filo together between the filling with the side of your hand, then cut into squares. Trim to make small parcels. Seal the edges, then brush with butter again.

4 Bake at 200°C (400°F) mark 6 for 8-10 minutes. Serve warm or cold.

Walnut Biscuits with Stilton and Celery

35 calories per savoury Makes about 80

25 g (1 oz) walnut pieces
125 g (4 oz) butter
225 g (8 oz) plain white flour
salt
225 g (8 oz) Stilton or any crumbly blue cheese
4 sticks of celery, finely chopped
1 bunch chives, snipped

1 Toast the walnuts and roughly chop. Rub the butter into the flour until it resembles fine breadcrumbs, then add the walnuts and a pinch of salt. Add 45-60 ml (3-4 tbsp) cold water and mix to form a dough. Knead lightly, then wrap and chill for 30 minutes.

2 Meanwhile, crumble the Stilton and mash with a fork. Stir the celery and chives into the cheese, reserving a few chives for the garnish, if wished. Cover and refrigerate.

3 On a floured surface, thinly roll out the pastry. Cut out 4 cm (1½ in) circles or any Christmas shapes. Re-roll the trimmings as necessary. Place on greased baking sheets. Bake at 180°C (350°F) mark 4 for about 10-15 minutes until golden. Cool on a wire rack.

4 Serve topped with a little of the Stilton mixture. Garnish with reserved chives, if wished.

Baked New Potatoes with Soured Cream and Bacon

180 calories per serving Serves 20 as part of a buffet

1.4 kg (3 lb) small new potatoes
salt and pepper
50 ml (2 fl oz) olive oil
275 g (10 oz) smoked rindless streaky bacon
300 ml (10 fl oz) soured cream
200 g (7 oz) low-fat soft cheese

1 Wash the potatoes, but do not peel them. Cook in a pan of boiling, salted water for 5 minutes, then drain well.

2 In a roasting tin, toss the potatoes with the oil. Bake at 200°C (400°F) mark 6 for about 35 minutes. Stir halfway through the cooking time. Drain on absorbent kitchen paper, then leave to cool for 10 minutes.

3 Meanwhile, grill the bacon until crisp. Drain on absorbent kitchen paper. In a food processor, blend the soured cream, soft cheese and bacon. Season. Pile the potatoes onto a platter and spear with cocktail sticks. Serve with the dip.

Mini Florentines

Cheese Croustades with Aubergine

80 calories per savoury Makes 48

12 large slices of white bread
about 125 g (4 oz) butter, melted
50 g (2 oz) freshly grated Parmesan
45 ml (3 tbsp) olive oil
2 shallots, skinned and finely chopped
225 g (8 oz) aubergine, finely diced
salt and pepper
350 g (12 oz) Stilton, crumbled
150 g (5 oz) plain fromage frais
60 ml (4 tbsp) snipped chives
snipped chives, to garnish

1 Cut the crusts off the bread and cut each slice into four squares.

2 Brush a patty tin with a little melted butter and firmly press a bread square into each hollow. Liberally brush the squares with butter and sprinkle with Parmesan.

3 Bake at 200°C (400°F) mark 6 for about 10-12 minutes until golden brown and crisp. Cool on a wire rack and store in an airtight container.

4 Heat the oil in a pan and sauté the shallots and aubergine until slightly softened, stirring frequently. Season well, cool.

5 Mix the Stilton with the fromage frais, keeping plenty of lumps of blue cheese. Season with pepper. Mix in the chives. Place the croustades on heatproof serving dishes and fill with the cheese mixture. Top with a little aubergine.

6 Warm in the oven at 200°C (400°F) mark 6 for 4-5 minutes. Scatter the chives over the top to garnish.

Mini Florentines

15 calories per Florentine (without chocolate)
Makes about 74

25 g (1 oz) walnut pieces
25 g (1 oz) flaked almonds
15 ml (1 tbsp) sultanas
15 ml (1 tbsp) chopped mixed candied peel
15 g (½ oz) glacé cherries
50 g (2 oz) butter
50 g (2 oz) caster sugar
15 ml (1 tbsp) double cream
125 g (4 oz) plain chocolate (optional)

1 Finely chop the nuts, sultanas, peel and cherries, then mix together. Grease some baking sheets.

2 Melt the butter in a saucepan, add the sugar and stir over a gentle heat until the sugar dissolves. Bring to the boil and boil for 1 minute. When the mixture turns a light golden colour, take off the heat and stir in the fruit, nuts and cream.

3 Place tiny amounts (no more than 2.5 ml (½ tsp)) on baking sheets, flattening slightly. Bake at 180°C (350°F) mark 4 for 5-6 minutes until golden. Leave to cool for 1 minute, then ease off the baking sheet, using a fish slice or spatula, and place on a wire rack to cool and harden.

4 If using, melt the chocolate, cool slightly, then brush onto one side of each Florentine. When hard, place in an airtight container, layered with greaseproof paper.

TAPAS PARTY

These delicious tapas, little dishes of Spain, consumed with great gusto at bars and taverns before lunch and again before dinner, have been a tradition in Spain for as long as anyone can remember.

Leek and Asparagus Vinaigrette

Saffron Aioli

Mixed Pepper Salad

Devilled Prawns

Roasted Potatoes with Shallots and Rosemary

Warm Spiced Aubergine and Mushroom Salad

Cheese Bites

Chorizo Puffs

Marinated Trout Fillets

Spanish Meatballs with Almond Saffron Sauce

Feta Cheese and Garlic Dip

Chicken Pinchitos

Almond Sweetmeats

Tapas represent a style of eating and a way of life that are so very Spanish and yet so adaptable. The possibilities are endless but here are some easy to prepare and delicious tapas recipes and ideas. As themed parties are very popular why not have a tapas party next time you are entertaining. Serve about eight tapas, choosing your own selection from the following recipes.

Fresh fruit ends most Spanish meals and as oranges are almost the symbol of Spain why not serve thinly sliced sweet oranges sprinkled with a few spoonfuls of dry sherry. Offer the Almond Sweetmeats with coffee.

Countdown

FOUR TO FIVE DAYS BEFORE
Make Aioli, cover and keep in refrigerator.

TWO DAYS BEFORE
Prepare Feta Cheese and Garlic Dip to end of step 2. Cover and chill. Stir gently before using. Prepare Mixed Pepper Salad, without basil, cover and keep in refrigerator. Bring to room temperature before serving, then add basil. Prepare Marinated Trout Fillets to end of step 3.

THE DAY BEFORE
Prepare Chicken Pinchitos to end of step 1. Cook when required. Make Almond Sweetmeats.

ONE HOUR BEFORE
Start preparing Roasted Potatoes with Shallots and Rosemary. Prepare Warm Spiced Aubergine and Mushroom Salad. Prepare Leek and Asparagus Vinaigrette. Cover and chill.

20 MINUTES BEFORE
Prepare Devilled Prawns. Complete any remaining finishing.

ALTERNATIVE CATERING QUANTITIES

(Standard recipes serve 6)

For 25 people prepare about 200 servings

For 50 people prepare about 300 servings

For 100 people prepare about 500 servings

VITAL STATISTICS

Serve about eight different tapas at a party. Each recipe serves six so simply select the tapas you prefer and multiply up the quantities as necessary. Choose a selection of hot and cold tapas, and do remember that there is a lot of last minute preparation here so do recruit plenty of willing helpers. Always check how much oven space you will need when selecting the recipes to cook.

FREEZER NOTES

Open freeze, then wrap Cheese Bites at end of step 3. Cook from frozen. Open freeze, then wrap Chorizo Puffs at end of step 4. Cook from frozen. Using fresh, not previously frozen mince, pack and freeze Spanish Meatballs at end of step 2. Thaw at cool room temperature for about 4 hours; then complete. Make Almond Saffron Sauce, then cool, pack and freeze. Thaw overnight at cool room temperature, warm to serve.

Mixed Pepper Salad

Leek and Asparagus Vinaigrette

290 calories per serving

450 g (1 lb) small tender leeks, cleaned

225 g (8 oz) thin asparagus, trimmed

salt and pepper

6 quail or 2 hen eggs

1 egg yolk

15 ml (1 tbsp) Dijon mustard

45 ml (3 tbsp) white wine vinegar

25 ml (5 level tsp) sugar

150 ml (¼ pint) olive oil

30 ml (2 tbsp) capers

30 ml (2 tbsp) flat-leaf parsley sprigs

1 Slice the leeks and asparagus into 7.5 cm (3 in) lengths. Cook together in boiling salted water for 1-2 minutes. Plunge quickly into a bowl of cold water to set the bright green colour. Drain.

2 Cook the eggs in boiling water for 1-2 minutes for quails' eggs or 10 minutes for hens'. Cool a little, peel, halve and roughly chop.

3 Mix together the egg yolk, mustard, vinegar and sugar, then gradually whisk in the olive oil. Season.

4 Toss the asparagus and leeks in the dressing. Arrange in a serving dish and sprinkle over the egg, capers and parsley sprigs. Cover and chill.

Saffron Aioli

140 calories per 15 ml (1 tbsp)

30 ml (2 tbsp) white wine vinegar

pinch of saffron strands

2 egg yolks

1 clove garlic, skinned and crushed

300 ml (½ pint) olive oil

salt and pepper

1 Heat the vinegar in a small saucepan and bubble for 2 minutes. Add the saffron.

2 Place the egg yolks in a food processor with the saffron, vinegar and garlic. Blend for 4-5 seconds with the motor running, then slowly add the olive oil as for mayonnaise.

3 When all the oil has been added, the mixture should be the consistency of lightly whipped cream. Season well.

NOTE: Aioli will keep, covered in the refrigerator, for 4-5 days.

Mixed Pepper Salad

125 calories per serving

700 g (1½ lb) red and yellow peppers, mixed

60 ml (4 tbsp) olive oil

1 clove garlic, skinned and finely chopped

50 g (2 oz) pitted black olives

a few fresh basil leaves

salt and pepper

1 Remove the core and seeds from the peppers, but leave whole. Place in a roasting tin and drizzle with 30 ml (2 tbsp) of the olive oil.

2 Cook at 200°C (400°F) mark 6 for about 45 minutes or until softened and well charred. Remove the skin and thickly slice.

3 Mix the garlic with the pepper slices, remaining oil, olives, basil and seasoning. Serve immediately.

Devilled Prawns

200 calories per serving

15 ml (1 tbsp) olive oil

125 g (4 oz) onion, skinned and finely chopped

2 cloves garlic, skinned and crushed

1.25 ml (¼ tsp) black pepper

1.25 ml (¼ tsp) salt

2.5 ml (½ tsp) dried oregano

2.5 ml (½ tsp) dried thyme

15 ml (1 tbsp) paprika

60 ml (4 tbsp) dry sherry

150 ml (5 fl oz) double cream

400 g (14 oz) cooked, peeled large prawns

paprika, to garnish

1 Heat the oil in a frying pan and lightly fry the onion and garlic for 3-4 minutes.

2 Add the pepper, salt, oregano, thyme, paprika and sherry. Cook, stirring, for 1 minute.

3 Pour in the cream and bubble vigorously to reduce the sauce slightly.

4 Add the prawns and bring back to boiling point. Serve immediately. Sprinkle over a little paprika to garnish.

Roasted Potatoes with Shallots and Rosemary

210 calories per serving

900 g (2 lb) potatoes

salt and pepper

1 stem fresh rosemary or 15 ml (1 tbsp) dried

60 ml (4 tbsp) olive oil

150 g (5 oz) shallots, skinned and quartered

2 cloves garlic, skinned and finely sliced

1 Peel the potatoes and cut into 2.5 cm (1 in) pieces. Cook in a pan of boiling salted water until just tender. Meanwhile, strip the fresh rosemary off the stem.

2 Heat the oil in a roasting tin and add the drained, hot potatoes and rosemary. Cook at 200°C (400°F) mark 6 for about 35 minutes, turning occasionally.

3 Add the shallots and garlic and continue to cook for a further 10-15 minutes or until golden brown. Season and serve immediately.

Warm Spiced Aubergine and Mushroom Salad

255 calories per serving

700 g (1½ lb) aubergines

225 g (8 oz) oyster or shitake mushrooms

about 150 ml (¼ pint) olive oil

175 g (6 oz) onion, skinned and finely chopped

2.5 cm (1 in) piece fresh root ginger, peeled and finely chopped

1 clove garlic, skinned and crushed

15 ml (1 tbsp) ground cumin

15 ml (1 tbsp) ground coriander

juice of 1 lemon

60 ml (4 tbsp) fresh coriander leaves

salt and pepper

1 Peel the aubergines and cut into 2.5 cm (1 in) cubes. Cut the mushrooms into similar sized pieces.

2 Heat 60 ml (4 tbsp) of the oil in a large non-stick frying pan and fry the aubergine cubes in batches, stirring frequently until evenly brown, adding more oil as necessary (see Cook's Tip). Remove the aubergines from the pan onto absorbent kitchen paper.

3 Stir in the onion, ginger, garlic and spices. Cook, stirring, for 2 minutes. Add the mushrooms and cook, uncovered, for 5 minutes or until any liquid has evaporated.

4 Return the aubergines to the pan and stir over the heat for 2 minutes or until tender. Add the lemon juice and coriander leaves. Adjust seasoning and serve warm.

COOK'S TIP

Aubergines are like blotting paper and will absorb a huge amount of oil. To keep the oil to a minimum use a non-stick pan and stir the aubergines frequently to prevent sticking.

Cheese Bites

65 calories per serving Makes about 24

125 g (4 oz) firm goat's cheese or Mozzarella cheese

50 g (2 oz) sun-dried tomatoes in oil, drained

50 g (2 oz) capers

50 g (2 oz) can anchovy fillets

50 g (2 oz) olives, pitted

225 g (8 oz) puff pastry

butter, for greasing

50 g (2 oz) pesto sauce

salt and pepper

1 Cut the cheese into small dice. Roughly chop sun-dried tomatoes, capers and anchovies. Halve or quarter the olives.

2 Roll out the pastry thinly to 3 mm (⅛ in) and stamp out about twenty four circles using a 5 cm (2 in) round cutter. Place on a buttered baking sheet.

3 Arrange the olives, cheese, sun-dried tomatoes, capers and anchovies on each circle. Spoon over a little pesto sauce and season.

4 Cook at 200°C (400°F) mark 6 for 10-15 minutes until well risen and crisp. Serve immediately.

Chorizo Puffs

85 calories per serving Makes about 18

225 g (8 oz) puff pastry

1 egg

salt

125 g (4 oz) spicy chorizo or pepperoni sausage, finely diced

1 small bunch fresh basil, about 15 g (½ oz), roughly torn

butter, for greasing

poppy seeds or sesame seeds

1 Roll out the pastry thinly to 3 mm (⅛ in). Stamp out about eighteen circles using a 7.5 cm (3 in) round cutter.

2 Beat the egg with a pinch of salt and use to lightly brush each circle. Put 5 ml (1 tsp) chorizo and some torn basil leaves in the centre. Fold over to form a crescent shape and pinch the edges together.

3 Place on a greased baking sheet. Brush with the egg and sprinkle with poppy seeds or sesame seeds.

4 Cook at 200°C (400°F) mark 6 for 10-15 minutes until well risen and golden. Serve immediately.

Marinated Trout Fillets

265 calories per serving

---

50 g (2 oz) carrot, peeled
---
60 ml (4 tbsp) white wine vinegar
---
120 ml (8 tbsp) olive oil
---
125 g (4 oz) onion, skinned and finely sliced
---
350 g (12 oz) fresh trout fillet (see Cook's Tip)
---
salt and pepper

---

1 Cut the carrot into thin matchsticks. Gently heat the vinegar and oil together. Add the onion and carrot and simmer for 5 minutes.

2 Meanwhile to steam the trout, place a wire rack over a frying pan of gently simmering water. Lay the trout on the rack and cover with foil. Steam for 4-5 minutes or until just cooked.

3 Cool the trout, then skin and flake into large pieces. Place in a dish with the warm oil and vinegar mixture. Season. Cool, cover and refrigerate for several hours, preferably overnight. Spoon the liquid over the fish occasionally. Serve at room temperature.

Spanish Meatballs with Almond Saffron Sauce

50 calories per serving without sauce Makes about 30

---

50 g (2 oz) sliced white or brown bread, crusts removed
---
45 ml (3 tbsp) milk
---
175 g (6 oz) onion, skinned and finely chopped
---
450 g (1 lb) minced beef or lamb
---
1 clove garlic, skinned and crushed
---
15 ml (1 tbsp) dried thyme
---
30 ml (2 tbsp) chopped fresh parsley
---
5 ml (1 tsp) grated nutmeg
---
1 egg, beaten
---
salt and pepper
---
flour, for coating
---
30 ml (2 tbsp) olive oil
---
1 quantity Almond Saffron Sauce (see method)
---
lemon juice, to taste

---

1 Soak the bread in the milk for 5 minutes. Squeeze out the liquid and add the bread to the onion, mince, garlic, thyme, parsley, nutmeg, egg and seasoning.

2 Blend the mixture thoroughly, then shape into about thirty balls and dust lightly with flour.

3 Heat the oil in a large non-stick frying pan and fry the meatballs in batches until well browned. Drain on absorbent kitchen paper.

4 Prepare the Almond Saffron Sauce to end of step 3, adding an extra 150 ml (¼ pint) stock and using the pan in which the meatballs were fried.

5 Add the meatballs to the sauce, cover and simmer for about 25 minutes or until tender, stirring occasionally. Squeeze over the lemon juice just before serving.

Almond Saffron Sauce

200 calories per serving

---

25 g (1 oz) bread
---
30 ml (2 tbsp) olive oil
---
125 g (4 oz) almonds, whole and blanched
---
2 cloves garlic, skinned and crushed
---
pinch of ground saffron
---
pinch of ground cloves
---
salt and pepper
---
150 ml (¼ pint) white wine
---
300 ml (½ pint) chicken stock
---
juice of 1 lemon (optional)

---

1 Cut the bread into rough pieces. Heat the oil in a frying pan, preferably non-stick, and cook the almonds and bread over a low heat until evenly golden, stirring frequently.

2 Stir in the garlic, saffron, cloves, seasoning and wine. Allow to bubble for 1-2 minutes.

3 Put the almond mixture into a food processor, add half the stock and blend until almost smooth. Return to the frying pan along with remaining stock, bring back to the boil.

4 Cover the sauce and simmer for 25 minutes, stirring occasionally.

Spanish Meatballs

Feta Cheese and Garlic Dip

245 calories per serving

225 g (8 oz) feta cheese
125 ml (4 fl oz) olive oil
juice of 1 lemon
3 cloves garlic, skinned and crushed
5 ml (1 tsp) dried oregano
10 ml (2 tsp) chilli paste (see Cook's Tip)
30 ml (2 tbsp) finely chopped gherkins
freshly ground black pepper
chopped chilli and gherkins, to garnish
cherry tomatoes, caper berries and olives, to serve

1 Crumble the feta cheese into a food processor with the motor running, then gradually add all the oil and lemon juice.

2 Add the garlic, oregano and chilli paste and process for 1-2 minutes. Stir in the gherkins and adjust seasoning.

3 Garnish with chopped chilli and gherkins. Serve with *toastades* (see Cook's Tip), whole cherry tomatoes, caper berries and olives.

COOK'S TIPS

Chilli paste – chopped chillies mixed with oil – can be found in small jars in most supermarkets. Alternatively use 1 small, chopped and seeded red chilli.

Toastades are baked bite sized pieces of bread. Try sun-dried tomato bread.

Chicken Pinchitos

135 calories per serving

7.5 ml (1½ tsp) medium curry powder
7.5 ml (1½ tsp) ground cumin
5 ml (1 tsp) ground coriander
2.5 ml (½ tsp) ground turmeric
pinch of ground cinnamon
pinch of cayenne pepper
450 g (1 lb) chicken breast fillet or boned thigh
30 ml (2 tbsp) chopped fresh parsley
juice of 1 lemon
30 ml (2 tbsp) olive oil
5 spring onions, trimmed and roughly chopped
salt and pepper

1 Combine all the spices together in a bowl. Cut the chicken into bite-sized pieces. Mix with the spices, chopped parsley and lemon juice. Cover and refrigerate for at least 2 hours or overnight.

2 Heat the oil in a frying pan and fry the chicken in batches for 4-5 minutes or until tender, stirring frequently. Add the spring onions, and season. Serve hot.

Almond Sweetmeats

85 calories per sweetmeat Makes about 30

125 g (4 oz) toasted chopped almonds
200 g (7 oz) ground almonds
30 ml (2 tbsp) currants
pinch of ground cinnamon
grated rind of 1 lemon
200 g (7 oz) thick honey, warmed
icing sugar, to dust

1 Beat together the chopped almonds, ground almonds, currants, pinch of ground cinnamon and grated lemon rind with the warmed honey. Knead well.

2 While warm, shape into 30 small balls. Dust with sifted icing sugar and wrap in coloured tissue to serve.

Left:

Above: **Chicken Pinchitos;** centre: **Chorizo Puffs** (page 74)

Below: **Roasted Potatoes with Shallots and Rosemary** (page 74)

Right:

Above: **Feta Cheese and Garlic Dip accompanied by** *toastades*, **cherry tomatoes, caper berries and olives**

Centre: **Saffron Aioli** (page 73)

CHRISTMAS BUFFET

For easy Christmas entertaining, try these wonderful advance preparation dishes — for no last minute fuss!

Savoury Lasagnes

Spinach and Watercress Salad with Bacon

Sliced Tomato Salad

Olive and Walnut Bread

Orange and Blueberry Compote

Almond Torte

Serves 12

Buffet food, especially at this time of year, should be easy to serve and eat, so here are three recipes for lasagnes that can be frozen. Each one serves six people — to serve twelve, just double up one recipe, or prepare two different ones. The bread and the delicious compote and torte can also be made in advance, leaving simple final touches for the day of the party.

Countdown

TWO DAYS BEFORE
Make Orange and Blueberry Compote to end of step 3.
THE DAY BEFORE
Prepare lasagnes to end of step 6; cool, cover and refrigerate. Make Olive and Walnut Bread to end of step 6. Once cold, wrap and store in refrigerator. Prepare salad dressings; cover and store in a cool place. Make Almond Torte to end of step 5; cover and refrigerate.
TO SERVE AT 8PM
IN THE MORNING
Grill bacon for salad, snip up, cover and chill. Prepare spinach and watercress; refrigerate in polythene bags. Blanch asparagus or beans, slice tomatoes, arrange on a serving platter, cover and chill.
6.45pm Preheat oven to 200°C (400°F) mark 6.
7pm Bake lasagne(s).
7.30pm Wrap bread in foil and reheat for 15-20 minutes.
7.45pm Complete salads.
8pm Serve meal. Take torte out of refrigerator to come to room temperature.

ALTERNATIVE CATERING QUANTITIES

(Standard menu serves 12)

Guests	25	50	100
Seafood, Creamy Chicken or Leek and Mushroom Lasagne	x 4	x 7	x 14
Sliced Tomato Salad	x 2	x 4	x 7
Spinach and Watercress Salad with Bacon	x 2	x 4	x 7
Olive and Walnut Bread	x 2	x 3	x 5
Orange and Blueberry Compote	x 2	x 4	x 6
Almond Torte	x 2	x 4	x 6

VITAL STATISTICS

You will need plenty of oven space here.

Lasagnes

Resist the temptation to use too large dishes as the lasagne will take so long to heat through that it can become dried up on the outside. Cook the lasagnes in rotation so that they come out of the oven at regular intervals. Lasagnes do retain heat well and if uncut will still be hot after standing at room temperature for 20 minutes or more.

Olive and Walnut Bread

Allow the guests to slice their own bread as it will keep fresher that way.

Almond Torte

Just before serving divide into portions so that you have control over how much each guest takes!

FREEZER NOTES

Using fresh (not previously frozen) ingredients, prepare lasagne(s) to end of step 6; cool, overwrap and freeze. Thaw overnight at cool room temperature. Bake at 200°C (400°F) mark 6 for 1 hour or until piping hot and well browned. Prepare Olive and Walnut Bread to end of step 6. Cool completely, overwrap and freeze. Thaw overnight, still wrapped, at cool room temperature. Reheat at 200°C (400°F) mark 6 for 15-20 minutes, wrapped in foil. Pack and freeze compote at end of step 3. Thaw overnight at cool room temperature. Chill before serving. Pack and freeze torte after turning out, but before soaking in syrup. Thaw at cool room temperature for 4 hours, spoon over syrup. The salads will not freeze.

Seafood Lasagne

Seafood Lasagne

720 calories per serving Serves 6

450 g (1 lb) fresh haddock fillet, skinned

300 ml (½ pint) white wine

slices of carrot, onion and bay leaf, for flavouring

salt and pepper

oil

200 g (7 oz) lasagne verdi

150 g (5 oz) butter

450 g (1 lb) trimmed leeks, cleaned and thickly sliced

1 clove garlic, skinned and crushed

90 g (3½ oz) plain white flour

150 ml (5 fl oz) single cream

150 ml (5 fl oz) soured cream

15 ml (1 tbsp) chopped fresh dill or 2.5 ml (½tsp) dried dill weed

225 g (8 oz) ready-cooked seafood cocktail

50 g (2 oz) Cheddar or Gruyère cheese, grated

30 ml (2 tbsp) grated Parmesan cheese

45 ml (3 tbsp) pine nuts

1 Cover the haddock fillets with water and half the wine. Add the flavouring ingredients. Season and bring to the boil. Cover and simmer for 5 minutes or until tender.

2 Lift the fish onto a plate and flake the flesh, discarding any bones. Strain the cooking juices, then make up to 1 litre (1¾ pints) with water.

3 Cook the lasagne according to packet instructions, stirring occasionally with a fork. (Even if you are using no-cook lasagne, you should still boil it for about 7 minutes.) Drain and immediately run cold water over the pasta. Spread on a clean tea towel and cover with a damp tea towel until required.

4 Melt 50 g (2 oz) of the butter in a medium saucepan. Add the leeks and garlic, cover and cook gently for about 10 minutes. Remove from the pan using a slotted spoon.

5 Add the remaining 75 g (3 oz) butter to the pan and melt. Add the flour and cook, stirring, for 1 minute. Off the heat, mix in the reserved 1 litre (1¾ pints) of stock and remaining 150 ml (¼ pint) wine. Bring to the boil, stirring, and cook for 2 minutes. Off the heat, whisk in the cream, soured cream and dill. Season.

6 Spoon a little of the sauce into a 3 litre (5¼ pint) shallow ovenproof dish. Top with a layer of pasta, followed by the haddock, seafood cocktail and leeks, and a little more sauce. Continue layering the ingredients, finishing with the sauce. Scatter over the grated Cheddar cheese, Parmesan cheese and pine nuts.

7 Cook at 200°C (400°F) mark 6 for 45-50 minutes or until piping hot. Cool for 10 minutes before serving.

COOK'S TIP

Look out for packs of chilled or frozen seafood cocktail, available from major supermarkets. They usually include cooked mussels, squid, prawns and sometimes cockles. If you can't find them, simply replace with some cooked, peeled prawns

VARIATIONS

Creamy Chicken Lasagne

700 calories per serving

Ingredients as for Seafood Lasagne, replacing the haddock and seafood cocktail/prawns with 1.4 kg (3 lb) oven-ready chicken, and the dill with 60 ml (4 tbsp) chopped fresh basil or 5 ml (1 tsp) dried. Cover the chicken with water, half the wine and the flavourings as in step 1. Bring to the boil, cover and simmer for 1 hour or until tender. Cut the chicken into bite-sized pieces, discarding the skin and bone. Bubble down the cooking juices to about 1 litre (1¾ pints). Strain and skim. Complete the lasagne as in steps 3-7, whisking 30 ml (2 tbsp) Dijon mustard into the sauce in step 5. Alternatively, 450 g (1 lb) ready-cooked chicken or turkey could be used, making the sauce with the wine and 900 ml (1½ pints) good chicken stock.

Leek and Mushroom Lasagne

720 calories per serving

Ingredients as for Seafood Lasagne, replacing the haddock and seafood cocktail/prawns with 450 g (1 lb) mixed mushrooms (brown cap, flat, oyster, etc) and the dill with 60 ml (4 tbsp) chopped fresh basil or 5 ml (1 tsp) dried. Increase the leeks to 700 g (1½ lb) and Cheddar or Gruyère cheese to 225 g (8 oz). Omit steps 1-2. Continue as in steps 3-4, then sauté the sliced mushrooms in the remaining 75 g (3 oz) butter for 3-4 minutes; remove from the pan using slotted spoons. Make the sauce as in step 5, adding more butter if necessary and using 700 ml (1¼ pints) vegetable stock and 300 ml (½ pint) white wine with the basil in place of dill. Whisk in 30 ml (2 tbsp) Dijon mustard. Complete as in steps 6-7, layering the mushrooms and some of the Cheddar or Gruyère cheese in place of the fish.

Spinach and Watercress Salad with Bacon

135 calories per serving

225 g (8 oz) smoked streaky bacon
225 g (8 oz) young spinach leaves
2 bunches watercress
75 ml (5 tbsp) olive oil
15 ml (1 tbsp) hazelnut oil
20 ml (4 tsp) white wine vinegar
15 ml (1 tbsp) wholegrain mustard
salt and pepper

1 Grill the streaky bacon until really crisp. Drain on absorbent kitchen paper to absorb any excess oil. Snip into small pieces, discarding the rind.

2 Pick over the spinach and watercress leaves, discarding any coarse stalks. Rinse, drain and dry. Shred any large spinach leaves.

3 Whisk together both types of oil with the white wine vinegar, wholegrain mustard and seasoning.

4 Just before serving, toss all the ingredients together and serve in a large salad bowl.

COOK'S TIP
You can use a mixture of spinach and watercress leaves, as we have here, or keep to a simple watercress salad, using four bunches in all.

Sliced Tomato Salad

70 calories per serving

350 g (12 oz) asparagus tips or stick beans, trimmed
salt and pepper
a few sun-dried tomatoes (optional)
90 ml (6 tbsp) olive oil
25 ml (5 tsp) raspberry or red wine vinegar
5 ml (1 tsp) runny honey
1 shallot, skinned and finely chopped
about 1.1 kg (2½ lb) ripe beef tomatoes, thinly sliced

1 Halve the asparagus or beans, if wished, then blanch in boiling, salted water until just tender. Drain and refresh the vegetables under cold running water.

2 Shred the sun-dried tomatoes, if using. Whisk together with the oil, vinegar, honey, shallot and seasoning.

3 Just before serving, arrange the sliced tomatoes on a large serving platter. Pile the asparagus tips or stick beans in the centre. Spoon over the dressing.

Olive and Walnut Bread

125 calories per slice Makes two loaves (12 slices each)

125 g (4 oz) stoned black olives
75 g (3 oz) walnuts
600 g (1 lb 5 oz) plain white strong flour
10 ml (2 tsp) salt
7 g (¼ oz) sachet fast-action dried yeast
75 ml (5 tbsp) chopped fresh parsley
olive oil

1 Mix the olives and walnuts together with the flour, salt, yeast and parsley.

2 Make a well in the centre of the dry ingredients and add 375 ml (13 fl oz) tepid water mixed with 45 ml (3 tbsp) oil. Stir together to form a soft dough, adding water if necessary.

3 Turn the dough onto a well floured surface and knead well until it is smooth and elastic – about 10 minutes.

4 Divide the dough in half and shape each piece into a roll 18-20.5 cm (7-8 in) long. Place rolls of dough on separate oiled baking sheets and cover loosely with lightly oiled cling film.

5 Leave the dough in a warm place for 30-40 minutes or until doubled in size. Lightly slash the top of each loaf.

6 Bake at 220°C (425°F) mark 7 for 12 minutes. Lower the temperature to 180°C (350°F) mark 4 for a further 25 minutes or until well browned and sounding hollow when tapped. Leave to cool for a few minutes on wire racks. Serve warm, thickly sliced.

Orange and Blueberry Compote

120 calories per serving

225 g (8 oz) granulated sugar
150 ml (¼ pint) Grand Marnier
12 large oranges
450 g (1 lb) fresh or frozen blueberries
Greek natural yogurt or crème fraîche, to accompany

1 Place the sugar in a saucepan with 600 ml (1 pint) water. Heat gently until the sugar dissolves then bring to the boil and boil for 2 minutes. Remove from the heat; cool. Stir in the Grand Marnier.

2 Using a serrated knife and working over a bowl to catch all juices, cut away all peel and pith from the oranges. Carefully slice the oranges into rings, discarding all pips. Pick over the blueberries, rinse and drain.

3 Place the oranges and blueberries in the bowl and pour over the syrup. Cover and refrigerate for at least 24 hours.

4 Serve the compote with thin wedges of Almond Torte, using some of the syrup to soak the torte (see below). Accompany with natural yogurt or crème fraîche.

Almond Torte

280 calories per serving

125 g (4 oz) softened butter
125 g (4 oz) caster sugar
finely grated rind and juice of 1 orange
2 eggs, beaten
125 g (4 oz) ground almonds
175 g (6 oz) semolina
10 ml (2 tsp) baking powder
5 ml (1 tsp) almond essence
200 ml (7 fl oz) Grand Marnier syrup from Orange and Blueberry Compote
toasted ground almonds and icing sugar, to decorate

1 Grease and base-line a 21.5 cm (8½ in) base measurement moule à manqué (a sloping-sided cake tin, about 5 cm [2 in] deep), or a deep round cake tin with non-stick baking parchment.

2 Beat the softened butter, sugar and finely grated orange rind until light and fluffy. Gradually beat in the eggs.

3 Beat in the almonds, semolina, baking powder, almond essence and 30 ml (2 tbsp) orange juice until evenly blended. Spoon into the tin, carefully levelling the surface with the back of a spoon.

4 Bake at 220°C (425°F) mark 7 for 10 minutes, then lower the temperature to 180°C (350°F) mark 4 and continue baking for a further 25 minutes or until well browned and firm to the touch. A skewer inserted into the centre should come out clean.

5 Cool in the tin for 10-15 minutes, then turn out onto a plate and carefully spoon over the Grand Marnier syrup. Leave to cool.

6 To serve, sprinkle with toasted ground almonds and sifted icing sugar and cut into thin wedges. Accompany with the Orange and Blueberry Compote.

NOTE

The torte is soaked in syrup from the Orange and Blueberry Compote. Alternatively, simply make a syrup from 75 g (3 oz) sugar, 200 ml (7 fl oz) water and 60 ml (4 tbsp) Grand Marnier and spoon this over.

Almond Torte with Orange and Blueberry Compote

FESTIVE BUFFET

This elegant, mildly spicy buffet looks fabulously impressive.

Vegetable Crisps

Tomato and Chilli Salsa

Caramelized Duckling

Spiced Rice and Lentils

Citrus Leeks with Sugar-snap Peas

Golden Mascarpone Tarts

Pear Sauce

Serves 12

Hand around the Vegetable Crisps and Tomato and Chilli Salsa with drinks instead of a starter, then follow with the main course – fabulous Caramelized Duckling.

Countdown

THE DAY BEFORE
Prepare Vegetable Crisps, seal in airtight containers. Make Tomato and Chilli Salsa, cover and refrigerate. Prepare Caramelized Duckling to end of step 3. Cool; refrigerate overnight. Prepare Spiced Rice and Lentils without adding parsley. Cool, cover and refrigerate. Prepare citrus dressing for vegetables, cover and refrigerate. Prepare pastry cases for Golden Mascarpone Tarts to end of step 2. Cool, store in airtight containers. Prepare Pear Sauce; cool, cover and refrigerate. Prepare vegetables, refrigerate in polythene bags.

ON THE DAY
IN THE MORNING
Complete step 3 of Golden Mascarpone Tarts and whisk together filling, but don't assemble. If serving vegetables cold, complete and allow to cool at room temperature.

TO SERVE AT 8PM
5.50pm Cook Golden Mascarpone Tarts.

7pm Increase oven temperature to 200°C (400°F) mark 6. Place Spiced Rice and Lentils in a buttered dish, cover with foil and reheat in oven. Remove citrus dressing from refrigerator. Arrange Vegetable Crisps, keep covered in a basket. Pour Salsa into a serving dish and cover.

7.30pm Bring Caramelized Duckling to boil on hob and place in oven. If serving vegetables warm, put on to cook and keep warm. If serving cold, complete.

7.50pm Stir herbs and Parma ham into casserole, adjust seasoning. Stir parsley into rice. Keep warm.

8pm Serve menu. Put loosely covered Golden Mascarpone Tarts back into a low oven to warm through.

ALTERNATIVE CATERING QUANTITIES
(Standard recipes serve 12)

Guests	25	50	100
Vegetable Crisps	x 2	x 3	x 6
Tomato and Chilli Salsa	x 2	x 3	x 6
Caramelized Duckling	x 2	x 4	x 7
Spiced Rice and Lentils	x 2	x 4	x 6
Citrus Leeks with Sugar-snap Peas	x 2	x 3	x 5
Golden Mascarpone Tarts	x 2	x 3	x 6
Pear Sauce	x 2	x 4	x 7

VITAL STATISTICS
You will need plenty of oven space here.

Caramelized Duckling
Make this recipe in single batches to ensure even cooking and reduction of the sauce. Be sure to order the duckling in advance as butchers and supermarkets don't usually carry a very large stock.

Spiced Rice and Lentils
Reheat in the oven as directed or in the microwave. Double quantity can be reheated at one time provided that it is in a large shallow dish and well covered to prevent it drying out.

Citrus Leeks with Sugar-snap Peas
For large numbers it is easiest to serve this cold.

Golden Mascarpone Tarts
These can be made in two 24 cm (9½ in) round fluted flan tins in place of the tranche tins. Cut into slices for serving to ensure portion control.

FREEZER NOTES
Cool, pack and freeze Caramelized Duckling at end of step 3. Thaw overnight at cool room temperature. Bring to boil on hob, then reheat at 150°C (300°F) mark 2 for 50 minutes-1 hour. Stir in herbs and sautéed Parma ham and a little more stock, if necessary, 10 minutes before serving. Cool, pack and freeze pastry cases for Golden Mascarpone Tarts at end of step 2. Thaw overnight at cool room temperature. Cool, pack and freeze Pear Sauce at end of step 3. Thaw overnight at cool room temperature.

Tomato and Chilli Salsa with Vegetable Crisps

Vegetable Crisps

about 130 calories per 25 g (1 oz)

900 g (2 lb) parsnips
900 g (2 lb) sweet potatoes
oil for deep frying
salt
6 red chillis (see Cook's Tip)
paprika
Tomato and Chilli Salsa, to serve

1 Peel, then thinly slice the parsnips and sweet potatoes separately in a food processor. Keep completely covered in cold water until required.

2 In a deep fat fryer, heat the oil to 170°C (325°F). Drain the parsnips and dry thoroughly on absorbent kitchen paper. Fry in small batches for 2-3 minutes, turning occasionally, until crisp and golden brown. Drain on absorbent kitchen paper to remove excess oil; dust with salt.

3 Drop the chillies into the oil and fry the sweet potatoes with the chillies, as above. Drain on absorbent kitchen paper and dust with paprika.

4 Store separately in airtight containers for up to three days. To serve, pile into baskets, garnish with the deep-fried chillies. Serve with the Salsa.

COOK'S TIP
When preparing chillies, it is best to wear rubber gloves to prevent skin irritation.

Tomato and Chilli Salsa

40 calories per serving

900 g (2 lb) ripe tomatoes
6 anchovy fillets
10 ml (2 tsp) capers
1 small red chilli (see Cook's Tip)
15 g (½ oz) fresh white breadcrumbs
15 ml (1 tbsp) red wine vinegar
30 ml (2 tbsp) olive oil
5 ml (1 tsp) caster sugar
salt and pepper

1 Skin, seed and finely chop the tomatoes. Roughly chop the anchovies and capers. Halve, seed and finely chop the chilli.

2 Mix together with the breadcrumbs, vinegar, oil and sugar. Season to taste.

3 Blend half the mixture in a food processor until almost smooth. Stir into the remainder. Serve with the Vegetable Crisps.

Caramelized Duckling

310 calories per serving

olive oil
1.4 kg (3 lb) onions, skinned, halved and sliced
75 g (3 oz) soft light brown sugar
90 ml (6 tbsp) sherry vinegar
12 whole allspice berries
10 duckling breasts, about 1.8 kg (4 lb) total weight
50 g (2 oz) plain white flour
10 ml (2 tsp) paprika
salt and pepper
900 ml (1½ pints) chicken stock
20 ml (4 tsp) dry sherry
grated rind and juice of 1 lemon
10 ml (2 tsp) chopped fresh marjoram or 5 ml (1 tsp) dried
175 g (6 oz) Parma ham
flat-leaf parsley, to garnish

1 Heat 30 ml (2 tbsp) oil in a large flameproof casserole and sauté the onions, uncovered, for 20 minutes. Stir in the sugar, vinegar and allspice. Cook for about 5 minutes until caramelized and a rich brown.

2 Meanwhile, skin the duckling and cut into bite-sized pieces. Mix the flour and paprika; season. Coat the duckling in the flour.

3 Remove the onions and juices from the pan, rinse the pan and add 75 ml (5 tbsp) oil. Heat, then brown the duckling in batches, adding a little more oil if necessary. Drain on absorbent kitchen paper. Place all the duckling in the casserole with any remaining flour. Off the heat, stir in the stock with the onions, sherry, grated lemon rind and juice, and marjoram. Bring to the boil, cover and cook at 150°C (300°F) mark 2 for 50 minutes or until almost tender.

4 Lightly sauté the chopped Parma ham in 15 ml (1 tbsp) oil for 3-4 minutes. Stir into the duckling. Cover and cook for a further 10 minutes or until the duckling is tender. Season and garnish with flat-leaf parsley.

COOK'S TIP
It is important to brown the duckling meat well in hot oil. This seals the outside and gives good colour to the casserole. It is best to seal in small batches to stop the pieces sticking together too much. If you try sealing too much at one time, the pieces of duckling will begin to stew.

If you have to keep the casserole warm for a long time, it is best not to leave it on the hob as it may stick. It is best to keep casseroles warm in a low oven.

Top: **Spiced Rice and Lentils;**
Below: **Citrus Leeks with Sugar-snap Peas**

Citrus Leeks with Sugar-snap Peas

150 calories per serving

1.4 kg (3 lb) trimmed leeks, cleaned

45-60 ml (3-4 tbsp) olive oil

900 g (2 lb) sugar-snap peas or mangetout, trimmed

salt and pepper

125 ml (4 fl oz) olive oil

25 ml (1 fl oz) balsamic vinegar

5 ml (1 tsp) soft light brown sugar

15-30 ml (1-2 tbsp) lemon juice

5 ml (1 tsp) Dijon mustard

grated rind and juice of 1 orange

1 Cut the leeks into 1 cm (½ in) slices. Heat the oil in a large sauté pan and gently sauté the leeks for 5-6 minutes or until just tender. Cook the sugar-snap peas in boiling, salted water for 5 minutes. Drain, then mix with the leeks.

2 Mix together oil, vinegar, sugar, lemon juice, mustard and grated orange rind and juice. Season. Stir into the hot vegetables and serve hot or cold.

Spiced Rice and Lentils

230 calories per serving

45 ml (3 tbsp) olive oil

225 g (8 oz) onion, skinned and finely chopped

3 bay leaves

1 cinnamon stick

5 whole green cardamoms, split

5 ml (1 tsp) fennel seeds

225 g (8 oz) whole green lentils

50 g (2 oz) wild rice

600 ml (1 pint) light stock

salt and pepper

400 g (14 oz) long grain white rice

45 ml (3 tbsp) chopped fresh parsley

1 Heat the oil in a large saucepan and sauté the onion with the bay leaves, cinnamon stick, cardamoms and fennel seeds for 3-4 minutes until the mixture starts to turn brown.

2 Add the lentils, wild rice and stock with 1.4 litres (2½ pints) water and 12.5 ml (½ tsp) salt. Bring to the boil, cover and simmer gently for 15 minutes.

3 Add the white rice, bring back to the boil, cover and simmer for a further 10 minutes. Remove the lid and cook for a further 5 minutes, stirring occasionally.

4 Drain, remove the cinnamon stick and bay leaves. Stir in the parsley; season and serve.

Golden Mascarpone Tarts

450 calories per serving

350 g (12 oz) plain white flour

caster sugar

175 g (6 oz) unsalted butter

450 g (1 lb) pears

2 bananas

350 g (12 oz) fresh dates

40 g (1½ oz) butter

350 g (12 oz) mascarpone cheese

4 eggs, size 3

30 ml (2 tbsp) rum

2.5 ml (½ tsp) vanilla essence

soft dark brown sugar

Pear Sauce or single cream, to accompany

1 Mix together the flour and 150 g (5 oz) caster sugar. Rub in the unsalted butter until the mixture resembles breadcrumbs. Stir in 75-90 ml (5-6 tbsp) water. Gently knead the dough until smooth. Wrap and chill for 30 minutes.

2 Use the dough to line two 34 x 11.5 cm (13½ x 4½ in) loose-based, fluted tranche tins. Bake blind until dry and light golden (see Cook's Tip).

3 Peel, quarter and core the pears, slice the bananas, halve and stone the dates. Melt the 40 g (1½ oz) butter in a large, heavy-based saucepan, stir in the pears and dates, then sauté

for 3-4 minutes until beginning to soften. Add the bananas and cook for a further minute.

4 Divide the fruit between the tranche tins. Whisk together the mascarpone, eggs, rum and vanilla essence with 50 g (2 oz) caster sugar until smooth. Spoon over the fruit to cover. Sprinkle 30 ml (2 tbsp) dark brown sugar over each tin.

5 Bake at 170°C (325°F) mark 3 for about 35 minutes or until just set. Sprinkle over a little more soft dark brown sugar. Flash under a hot grill to caramelize the sugar. Serve warm with Pear Sauce or single cream.

COOK'S TIPS

Italian mascarpone cheese is rich and creamy. If you can't find it, beat together 200 g (7 oz) full-fat soft cheese with 150 ml (5 fl oz) single cream. The mixture will set a little firmer, but will be just as delicious. If you don't like cooked bananas, use another pear instead.

To bake blind, chill the pastry case well. Prick the base well, then line the pastry case with greaseproof paper and baking blind beans. Bake at 200°C (400°F) mark 6 for about 10 minutes until just set. Remove the baking beans and paper and return the pastry case to the oven for a further 10 minutes.

Pear Sauce

60 calories per serving

125 g (4 oz) caster sugar

pared rind and juice of 1 lemon

450 g (1 lb) ripe, firm pears

1 Place the sugar and pared lemon rind in a heavy-based saucepan with 350 ml (12 fl oz) water. Dissolve over a gentle heat.

2 Peel, quarter, core and roughly chop the pears. Add to the sugar syrup. Bring to the boil and simmer gently for about 5 minutes or until just softened.

3 Blend in a food processor, then sieve and stir in 15 ml (1 tbsp) lemon juice. Serve cold with the Golden Mascarpone Tarts.

Golden Mascarpone Tart

TRADITIONAL CHRISTMAS LUNCH

A perfectly planned menu to give you and your family the gloriously memorable Christmas lunch that everyone always longs for.

Carpaccio of Salmon

Bacon-roasted Turkey

Sage, Apple and Onion Stuffing

Crispy Roast Potatoes

Sprouts in Hazelnut Butter

Pan-fried Carrots

Creamy Bread Sauce

Cranberry and Apple Relish

Traditional Christmas Pudding and Brandy Butter or

Mango and Rum Trifle

Serves 10

Advance preparation is the key to a successful Christmas lunch. The detailed countdown will be of particular help at this busy time of year. Do read the Turkey Tips on thawing, stuffing, cooking and testing, and refer to the turkey timetable for a succulent, perfectly cooked turkey.

Countdown

Before you start, check the menu and ensure that you have sufficient space in your oven for all the dishes. If not, adapt the menu accordingly.

EARLY NOVEMBER
Make Christmas Pudding.

ONE WEEK BEFORE CHRISTMAS
Prepare Cranberry and Apple Relish. Calculate thawing time of turkey (see chart) and thaw on right day. Make Brandy Butter.

23 DECEMBER
Make Creamy Bread Sauce to end of step 2, cover and chill. Prepare Hazelnut Butter, cover and chill.

CHRISTMAS EVE
Bat out salmon, leave between sheets of cling film, cover and refrigerate. Prepare tomato dressing, cover and refrigerate separately. Make Sage, Apple and Onion Stuffing (if using). Prepare stock for gravy: simmer giblets in a covered pan with 1.1 litres (2 pints) water, seasoning and a few vegetables for 2 hours or until about 600 ml (1 pint) stock remains. Strain, cool and refrigerate. Pare carrots, cover with cold water and chill. Prepare sprouts; refrigerate in a polythene bag. Make Mango and Rum Trifle to end of step 4. Whip cream for trifle, cover and refrigerate separately.

CHRISTMAS DAY
Times given are for a 5-5.4 kg (11-12 lb) oven-ready turkey. Calculate cooking time to allow the turkey to sit and relax for 30 minutes before carving. Times given are to serve lunch at 1pm (Or dinner at 7pm).

8.15am (2.15pm) Preheat oven to 190°C (375°F) mark 5. Stuff turkey and complete recipe ready to roast.

8.45am (2.45pm) Put turkey in oven to cook.

10.30am (4.30pm) Put relish in serving dish. Take dressing for Carpaccio out of refrigerator. Cut slices of bread and butter, cover bread tightly. Put Traditional Christmas Pudding on to steam.

11.15am (5.15pm) Blanch potatoes and put in oven to roast; baste them occasionally.

11.45am (5.45pm) Unwrap turkey and return to oven. Grill spicy sausages. Put extra stuffing into the oven to bake.

12.15pm (6.15pm) Spoon tomato dressing over salmon and leave in a cool place.

12.30pm (6.30pm) Test turkey thigh with a skewer. Tent turkey with foil to keep warm. Make gravy. Raise oven to 220°C (425°F) mark 7 and complete potatoes; keep warm, uncovered. Cook sprouts, fry carrots. Cover and keep warm. Reheat bread sauce and add cream. Cook the Carpaccio for 5 minutes, if wished.

1pm (7pm) Serve the meal. Take Brandy Butter out of refrigerator about 30 minutes before serving. Decorate trifle just before serving. Turn out Traditional Christmas Pudding to serve.

ALTERNATIVE CATERING QUANTITIES

(Standard recipes serve 10)

Guests	25	50	100
Carpaccio of Salmon	x 2	x 4	x 8
Bacon-roasted Turkey	x 2	x 4	x 7
Sage, Apple and Onion Stuffing	x 2	x 4	x 7
Crispy Roast Potatoes	x 2½	x 4½	x 9
Sprouts in Hazelnut Butter	x 2	x 4	x 8
Pan-fried Carrots (see below)	x 1	x 2	x 3
Creamy Bread Sauce	x 2	x 4	x 8
Perfect Gravy	x 2	x 4	x 8
Cranberry and Apple Relish	x 2	x 4	x 7
Mango and Rum Trifle	x 2	x 4	x 8
Christmas Pudding	x 2	x 4	x 7
Brandy Butter	x 3	x 5	x 8

VITAL STATISTICS

Cooking Christmas Lunch for large numbers is a daunting task. Ensure you have masses of oven space, time and helpers. For more than fifty people we suggest you serve cold turkey (see Ballontine of Turkey on page 134) and accompany it with salads. The ballontine recipe can also be served hot; and being boned is easier to carve.

Carpaccio of Salmon
Spoon over the dressing at the last minute as the salmon quickly loses its colour.

Bacon-roasted Turkey
Never try to cook too large a turkey in a small oven as the heat won't circulate and the bird won't cook properly. Our quantity guide is based on a 5 kg (11 lb) oven-ready turkey as in the recipe. If you wish to cook larger birds check the chart for quantities and for cooking times.

Pan-fried Carrots
It is difficult to prepare these in very large quantities. Just serve a few as a garnish.

Puddings
Serve either the Traditional Christmas Pudding or the Mango and Rum Trifle, or try the Iced Christmas Pudding (see page 137).

FREEZER NOTES

Thaw turkey as directed. Freeze Creamy Bread Sauce at end of step 2; thaw overnight at cool room temperature; reheat. Freeze relish; thaw overnight at cool room temperature. Pack and freeze Hazelnut Butter for sprouts; thaw for 4 hours at cool room temperature. Freeze Christmas Pudding after maturing for one month. Thaw overnight at cool room temperature; reheat as in step 4. Pack and freeze Brandy Butter; thaw overnight in refrigerator.

Carpaccio of Salmon

200 calories per serving

600 g (1¼ lb) salmon fillet, skinned
125 ml (4 fl oz) olive oil
225 g (8 oz) tomatoes
1 bunch fresh chives or spring onions, trimmed
juice of 2 limes
salt and pepper
lime wedges, to garnish
slices of brown bread and butter, to accompany

1 Cut the salmon into twenty slices. Bat out thinly between sheets of oiled cling film. It should be the thickness of sliced smoked salmon.

2 Halve and seed the tomatoes, then finely chop the flesh. Chop the chives or spring onions into long pieces. Mix the chopped tomatoes and chives or spring onions with the lime juice, olive oil and seasoning.

3 Just before serving, arrange the salmon on individual serving plates and spoon the dressing over. Garnish with lime wedges and accompany with slices of brown bread and butter.

VARIATIONS

If the idea of eating raw salmon doesn't really appeal to you, place the Carpaccio of Salmon in single layers in ovenproof dishes. Cook at 220°C (425°F) mark 7 for about 5 minutes or until the salmon just turns opaque. Serve warm, garnished with lime. Alternatively, serve smoked salmon or gravadlax.

TURKEY TIPS

Thawing Frozen turkeys must be thoroughly thawed before cooking. They should be left in their bags and thawed at cool room temperature, not in the refrigerator. Remove giblets as soon as they are loose — these can be used to make stock for the gravy. To check the bird is completely thawed, make sure there are no ice crystals in the body cavity and that the legs are quite flexible. Once the bird is thoroughly thawed, cover and store in the refrigerator. Cook as soon as possible.

Stuffing Loosely stuff neck end only, to ensure heat penetrates more quickly. Extra stuffing can be baked separately in a covered dish for about 1 hour. Allow about 225 g (8 oz) stuffing for each 2.3 kg (5 lb) dressed weight of bird and stuff just before cooking. Sew up the neck skin or use skewers; truss the bird.

Cooking Weigh bird after stuffing and calculate the complete cooking time to be ready 30 minutes before carving; this allows the flesh to firm up, making carving much easier. Spread with butter or margarine, grind over black pepper or see Bacon-roasted Turkey. Wrap loosely in foil or put straight into a roasting tin in the oven at 190°C (375°F) mark 5. Fold back the foil about 45 minutes before the end of calculated cooking time to brown. Baste turkey regularly.

Testing Insert a skewer into a thigh. If juices run clear, it is cooked, otherwise return to the oven for a while longer.

NOTE

Leftover turkey should always be left to cool in a cold place, then refrigerated. Do not leave to stand in a warm room.

TURKEY TIMETABLE

Oven-ready weight (at room temperature)	Approx. hours thawing time	Cooking time, foil-wrapped (hours)	Approx. no. of servings
550 g-1.4 kg (1¼-3 lb)	4-10	1-1½	2-4
1.4-2.3 kg (3-5 lb)	10-15	1½-2	4-6
2.3-3.6 kg (5-8 lb)	15-18	2-3	6-10
3.6-5 kg (8-11 lb)	18-20	3-3½	10-15
5-6.8 kg (11-15 lb)	20-24	3½-4½	15-20
6.8-9 kg (15-20 lb)	24-30	4½-5	20-30

Carpaccio of Salmon

Bacon – roasted Turkey

400 calories per serving

1 quantity Sage, Apple and Onion Stuffing
1 oven-ready turkey, about 5 kg (11 lb)
125 g (4 oz) butter, softened
salt and pepper
350 g (12 oz) rindless, smoked streaky bacon rashers
about 450 g (1 lb) spicy sausages, to accompany

1 Spoon some of the stuffing into the neck end of the turkey only. Shape into a neat rounded end, then tuck the neck skin under the bird and secure firmly with a small skewer or wooden cocktail stick. (Place the remaining stuffing in a buttered ovenproof dish, cover with buttered foil.) Weigh the turkey and calculate the cooking time (see Turkey Timetable).

2 Place one or two large sheets of strong foil across a large roasting tin. Put the turkey in the middle and spread all over with the butter. Season with a little salt and plenty of freshly ground black pepper. Overlap the bacon rashers across the turkey.

3 Fold the sheets of foil loosely around the turkey to enclose it in a 'tent', leaving plenty of air space around the bird.

4 Cook at 190°C (375°F) mark 5 for about 3 hours. Fold back the foil and push the bacon slices off the breast to allow the skin to brown. Cook for a further 30-45 minutes basting frequently, or until tender. Grill the spicy sausages.

5 Lift the turkey from the roasting tin. Tip the bird slightly to allow the juices to run out, then place on a warmed serving dish. Cover with foil; leave to relax for 30 minutes to make carving easier. Serve with bacon and sliced spicy sausages. Meanwhile, prepare the Perfect Gravy.

COOK'S TIP

Test the turkey to make sure it is cooked through. Pierce the thickest part of the leg with a skewer: the juices will run clear if the bird is cooked — there should be no pink tinge. Pull one leg; it should easily give if the turkey is cooked.

Sage, Apple and Onion Stuffing

55 calories per 15 ml (1 tbsp)

175 g (6 oz) cooking apple
50 g (2 oz) butter
225 g (8 oz) onion, skinned and finely chopped
10 ml (2 tsp) dried sage
juice of 1 small lemon
700 g (1½ lb) pork sausagemeat
50 g (2 oz) fresh white breadcrumbs
salt and pepper

1 Peel, quarter, core and roughly chop the apple. Melt the butter in a pan and fry the apple and onion for 8-10 minutes or until softened and golden. Stir in the sage.

2 Mix with the lemon juice, sausagemeat and fresh white breadcrumbs. Season well. Cover and chill until required.

Crispy Roast Potatoes

290 calories per serving

1.8 kg (4 lb) old potatoes
coarse sea salt
150 ml (¼ pint) oil

1 Cut the potatoes into large chunks, leaving the skin on. Cover with cold, salted water, bring to the boil and simmer for 2-3 minutes.

2 Meanwhile, put the oil in a large, heavy-based roasting tin and heat in the oven at 190°C (375°F) mark 5 for about 5 minutes or until the oil is really hot.

3 Drain the potatoes, then cover the pan and shake to roughen up the surface of the potatoes.

4 Using an oven glove, place the roasting tin of hot oil over a medium heat on the hob. Carefully spoon in the hot potatoes and baste with the oil. Roast high in the oven for about 1 hour, basting occasionally. Turn up the heat to 220°C (425°F) mark 7 for a further 30 minutes to brown and crisp. Serve as soon as possible, sprinkled with coarse sea salt.

COOK'S TIPS

Make sure the potatoes are still hot when they go into the hot oil. This ensures that the outsides seal and become crispy and not greasy.

The potatoes can be peeled before cooking, but you will find potatoes roasted in their skins are golden and crispy with a wonderfully earthy flavour.

Traditional Christmas Lunch

Sprouts in Hazelnut Butter

120 calories per serving

75 g (3 oz) hazelnuts

75 g (3 oz) unsalted butter, softened

salt and pepper

grated nutmeg

1 clove garlic, skinned and crushed

grated rind of 1 lemon

1.4 kg (3 lb) Brussels sprouts

1 Toast the hazelnuts under the grill and roughly chop. Beat into the butter with seasoning, a little grated nutmeg, garlic and grated lemon rind.

2 Cook the sprouts in boiling, salted water for about 7-10 minutes or until tender but still retaining some of their bite. Drain well and toss in the hazelnut butter. Serve as soon as possible.

COOK'S TIP

If you prefer fresh chestnuts, buy about 175 g (6 oz) to allow for wastage. Nick the brown outer skins with a sharp knife. Cook in boiling water for 10 minutes. Drain, cool and peel off the shells and inner skins. Cover with stock and simmer for 20 minutes or until tender. Drain well. Toast, chop and use as hazelnuts above. Or, look for prepared frozen or vacuum-packed chestnuts in good delicatessens.

Pan-fried Carrots

35 calories per serving

450 g (1 lb) carrots, peeled

30 ml (2 tbsp) oil

salt and pepper

1 Pare the carrots into wafer-thin strips. Plunge into cold water until required. Drain well and pat dry.

2 Heat the oil and brown half the carrot strips for 3-4 minutes. Cover and keep warm while frying the remainder. Season and serve.

Creamy Bread Sauce

200 calories per serving

125 g (4 oz) onion, skinned

6 whole cloves

900 ml (1½ pints) milk

2 bay leaves

6 black peppercorns

salt and pepper

175 g (6 oz) fresh white breadcrumbs

75 g (3 oz) butter

60 ml (4 tbsp) double cream

chopped fresh parsley, to garnish

1 Halve the onion and stick in the cloves. Place in a pan with the milk, bay leaves, peppercorns and seasoning. Bring to the boil. Remove from the heat, cover and leave to infuse for 1 hour.

2 Strain the milk and return to the pan. Over a low heat, gradually add the breadcrumbs. Bring to the boil, stirring. Simmer for 2-3 minutes or until the sauce thickens slightly. Stir in the butter; season.

3 Just before serving, gently fold in the double cream. Garnish with some chopped fresh parsley.

Perfect Gravy

When the turkey is cooked, lift it on to a warmed serving dish. Pour any liquid from foil back into the tin. Tilt the tin to run the liquid into one corner. Spoon off all but 30 ml (2 tbsp) of the liquid fat, leaving the turkey juices behind. Place the tin over a low heat and add 30 ml (2 tbsp) plain flour. Stir in with a wooden spoon and cook for 1-2 minutes. Don't worry if it is lumpy at this stage. Slowly stir in 600 ml (1 pint) turkey stock. Bring to the boil, then simmer for 3-4 minutes or until you have a smooth, thin gravy; whisk if necessary to make it smooth. Off the heat, add 30 ml (2 tbsp) dry sherry and season to taste. Strain into a warmed gravy boat to serve.

Cranberry and Apple Relish

15 calories per 15 ml (1 tbsp)

350 g (12 oz) cooking apples

225 g (8 oz) cranberries

30 ml (2 tbsp) cider vinegar

225 g (8 oz) demerara sugar

2.5 ml (½ tsp) ground mixed spice

grated rind of 1 orange

1 Peel, core and slice the apples. Place in a large saucepan with the cranberries, vinegar, sugar, spice and orange rind.

2 Simmer for 20 minutes or until the fruit is pulpy, stirring occasionally.

3 Cool the cranberry and apple relish, cover and refrigerate for up to one week.

Traditional Christmas Pudding

445 calories per serving

50 g (2 oz) each blanched almonds, walnuts and Brazil nuts
75 g (3 oz) carrots, peeled
75 g (3 oz) pitted no-soak prunes
125 g (4 oz) butter
finely grated rind of 1 lemon
125 g (4 oz) soft dark brown sugar
2 eggs, beaten
350 g (12 oz) seedless raisins, currants and sultanas, mixed
25 g (1 oz) chopped mixed candied peel
50 g (2 oz) fresh brown breadcrumbs
125 g (4 oz) plain wholemeal flour
50 g (2 oz) plain white flour
15 ml (1 tbsp) ground mixed spice
200 ml (7 fl oz) Guinness
30 ml (2 tbsp) brandy
30 ml (2 tbsp) black treacle
about 10 silver coins, to serve (optional)
Brandy Butter, to accompany, and brandy, to serve

1 Roughly chop all the nuts, coarsely grate the carrots and snip the prunes into small pieces. Beat the butter and finely grated lemon rind until soft. Gradually beat in the sugar, followed by the eggs. Mix in all the remaining ingredients, stirring well. Cover and leave in a cool place overnight (not the refrigerator).

2 The next day, lightly grease a 1.4-1.6 litre (2½-2¾ pint) heatproof pudding basin and base-line with non-stick baking parchment. Beat the pudding mixture again and spoon it into the basin. Pleat a piece of greased greaseproof paper and foil together, and then tie this securely over the pudding basin.

3 Steam the pudding for about 6 hours. Alternatively, stand the basin in a large saucepan filled with enough boiling water to come halfway up the sides of the basin. Cover and boil for about 4 hours. Cook the pudding completely, re-cover the basin with fresh greaseproof paper and foil, and refrigerate for up to 2 months.

4 On the day, steam the pudding for about 3 hours or boil for about 2 hours. Turn out on to a warm serving plate. Warm about 60 ml (4 tbsp) brandy in a small saucepan, pour over the pudding and set alight. Baste with the flaming brandy, then serve, cut into wedges, with silver coins if wished, and accompanied by Brandy Butter.

Mango and Rum Trifle

Brandy Butter

190 calories per serving

125 g (4 oz) unsalted butter
125 g (4 oz) icing sugar, sifted
25 g (1 oz) ground almonds
30 ml (2 tbsp) brandy
60 ml (4 tbsp) double cream

1 Cream the butter. Gradually beat in the icing sugar, ground almonds and brandy.

2 Gently stir in the double cream, cover and refrigerate. Remove from the refrigerator 30 minutes before serving.

Mango and Rum Trifle

465 calories per serving

40 g (1½ oz) custard powder
75 g (3 oz) coconut milk powder
40 g (1½ oz) caster sugar
900 ml (1½ pints) milk
300 ml (10 fl oz) single cream
125 g (4 oz) macaroons or almond ratafias
150 ml (¼ pint) dark rum
400 g (14 oz) sponge cake such as Madeira
2 medium mangoes
6 passion fruit
150 ml (¼ pint) fresh orange juice
300 ml (10 fl oz) double cream
gold dragées, to decorate

1 Mix together the custard powder, coconut milk powder and caster sugar in a medium saucepan. Stir in a little of the milk, enough to make a smooth paste. (Whisk if necessary.)

2 Over a low heat, gradually add the remaining milk and single cream to the coconut paste mixture. Bring to the boil, stirring continuously, then simmer for 4-5 minutes until the custard is thickened and smooth; cool slightly.

3 Put the macaroons or ratafias in a large, deep, glass serving dish. Carefully drizzle over half the rum. Pour half the custard over the macaroons to cover them completely and leave to cool for about 15 minutes.

4 Trim the sponge to fit the bowl. Place on top of the custard. Peel, stone and roughly chop the mangoes. Mix with the passion fruit pulp, reserving 60 ml (4 tbsp) for decoration. Stir the orange juice and remaining rum into the fruit mixture and spoon over the sponge. Top with the remaining custard. Cool, cover, then chill, preferably overnight.

5 Whip the double cream very lightly until it just holds its shape. Spoon over the custard, piling it up a little in the centre. Decorate with the reserved mango and passion fruit and golden dragées.

NEW YEAR DINNER

A succulent lamb or pork roast and the season's finest ingredients produce a traditional menu full of surprises.

Creamy Carrot and Celeriac Soup

Herb Croûtons

Roast Lamb or Pork Fillet with Garlic and Rosemary

Leek and Honey Sauce

Golden Potatoes

Baked Tomato and Fennel

Caramelized Apple Wafers

Cinnamon Custard

Serves 6

A first-class meal to welcome the New Year. Fresh seasonal ingredients are simply cooked to make the most of their flavours.

Much of this menu can be made ahead, so that the main course needs only last-minute attention. The Creamy Carrot and Celeriac Soup can be frozen and the crunchy Herb Croûtons can be prepared the day before.

There is a choice of lamb or pork fillet for the main dish, roasted with garlic and rosemary.

The prettiest of desserts, Caramelized Apple Wafers, is a fan of apple slices set in a heart of puff pastry and marzipan, served with Cinnamon Custard. These wafers can be prepared ahead or frozen in advance.

Countdown

TWO DAYS BEFORE
Prepare soup to end of step 4. Cool, cover and refrigerate.

THE DAY BEFORE
Make and grill Herb Croûtons. Cool, then store in an airtight container. Prepare lamb or pork to end of step 2. Make Leek and Honey Sauce. Cool, cover and refrigerate. Make and bake Caramelized Apple Wafers. Cool, cover and refrigerate. Make Cinnamon Custard; refrigerate as directed.

TO SERVE AT 8PM
6pm Place croûtons on a baking sheet, ready to reheat. Place Caramelized Apple Wafers on a separate baking sheet and cover loosely with foil, ready to reheat. Preheat oven to 200°C (400°F) mark 6. Prepare and roast potatoes.

6.30pm Prepare Baked Tomato and Fennel; put in oven to cook.

7pm Complete steps 3 and 4 of meat recipe, set aside.

7.30pm Put meat in to roast. Add cream to soup and reheat. Reheat croûtons. Reheat Leek and Honey Sauce. Check vegetables and keep warm, as directed.

8pm Serve soup. Add pan juices to leek sauce. Reheat Caramelized Apple Wafers at 200°C (400°F) mark 6 for 15 minutes.

FREEZER NOTES

Cool, pack and freeze soup at end of step 4. When required, thaw overnight at cool room temperature and complete. Cool, pack and freeze Caramelized Apple Wafers after baking but before dusting with icing sugar. Place frozen onto baking sheets, cover loosely with foil and reheat at 200°C (400°F) mark 6 for about 20 minutes. Pack and freeze Cinnamon Custard. When required, thaw for 6 hours, then blend, as custard has a slightly rough texture after freezing. Chill.

ALTERNATIVE CATERING QUANTITIES

(Standard recipes serve 6)

Guests	25	50	100
Creamy Carrot and Celeriac Soup	x 3	x 6	x 10
Herb Croûtons	x 3	x 5	x 8
Roast Lamb or Pork Fillet with Garlic and Rosemary	x 4	x 7	x 13
Leek and Honey Sauce	x 4	x 7	x 13
Golden Potatoes	x 4	x 7	x 13
Baked Tomato and Fennel	x 4	x 7	x 13
Caramelized Apple Wafers	x 4	x 8	x 16
Cinnamon Custard	x 4	x 8	x 16

VITAL STATISTICS

You will need a great deal of oven space here so ask friends and neighbours for their help.

Roast Lamb or Pork Fillet with Garlic and Rosemary
When cooking in large quantities don't try to brown the meat first. Simply place it in the roasting tin with a little hot fat and add 5 minutes to all the cooking times. Don't overcrowd the roasting tins or the meat won't cook through. Cook in rotation so that the meat comes out of the oven at 5-minute intervals.

Golden Potatoes
Don't be tempted to overload the roasting tins as the potatoes won't brown evenly.

Baked Tomato and Fennel
If you haven't space to cook this simply serve a fresh tomato salad tossed with French Dressing and fennel seeds.

Caramelized Apple Wafers
You will find that there are quite a lot of pastry trimmings from each batch of wafers. Carefully fold these up, don't screw them into a ball, wrap well and keep for use another day. The trimmings don't rise so evenly so are best not used for this recipe.

Creamy Carrot and Celeriac Soup

200 calories per serving

225 g (8 oz) onion, skinned

900 g (2 lb) carrots, peeled

900 g (2 lb) celeriac, peeled

30 ml (2 tbsp) oil

1.7 litres (3 pints) chicken stock

5 ml (1 tsp) soy sauce

finely grated rind and juice of 1 orange

300 ml (½ pint) single cream

salt and pepper

Herb Croûtons, and flat-leaved parsley, to garnish

1 Roughly chop the onion, carrots and celeriac together. Heat the oil in a large saucepan and sauté the vegetables for 5 minutes, stirring frequently. Add the chicken stock, bring to the boil, cover and then leave to simmer gently for 20 minutes.

2 Stir in the soy sauce, finely grated orange rind and 60 ml (4 tbsp) orange juice. Cover and simmer for 20 minutes.

3 Cool slightly, then blend in a food processor until smooth. For an extra-velvety texture, push through a sieve.

4 Stir in the cream and warm gently. Season; serve garnished with Herb Croûtons and flat-leaved parsley.

Herb Croûtons

125 calories per serving

50 g (2 oz) butter

30 ml (2 tbsp) chopped fresh coriander or parsley

5 medium slices of bread

1 Beat the butter until soft, then mix in the coriander or parsley. Spread one side of the bread slices with the butter mixture. Using a small cutter, stamp out croûtons, discarding the crusts.

2 Place on a baking sheet, butter side up, and grill until golden brown. Keep warm, uncovered.

COOK'S TIP

These croûtons can be made ahead ready to reheat and serve. Simply place on a baking sheet, uncovered, and warm through for a few minutes.

Roast Lamb or Pork Fillet with Garlic and Rosemary

300 calories per serving

2 large rosemary sprigs

three 275 g (10 oz) lamb or pork fillets

75 ml (5 tbsp) olive oil

8-10 cloves garlic, skinned

fresh rosemary, to serve

1 Strip the spiky rosemary leaves off the sprigs. Remove any large pieces of fat from the lamb or pork.

2 Place the meat, 45 ml (3 tbsp) olive oil, the whole garlic cloves and rosemary in a non-metallic dish, into which they just fit. Cover and leave to marinate overnight in the refrigerator.

3 Heat the remaining oil in a frying pan. Remove the meat and garlic from the marinade and toss quickly in the pan to brown on all sides.

4 Place the fillets and garlic cloves in a roasting tin with the fat from the pan. Spoon over the remaining marinade.

5 Roast at 200°C (400°F) mark 6 for about 15 minutes for rare lamb and about 20 minutes for medium lamb. Roast the pork for about 35 minutes. Serve on a bed of fresh rosemary surrounded by the garlic cloves.

Leek and Honey Sauce

about 100 calories per serving

40 g (1½ oz) butter

350 g (12 oz) trimmed leeks, cleaned and finely chopped

15 ml (1 tbsp) plain white flour

300 ml (½ pint) chicken stock

75 ml (5 tbsp) white wine

30 ml (2 tbsp) white wine vinegar

30 ml (2 tbsp) runny honey

30 ml (2 tbsp) chopped fresh parsley

salt and pepper

1 Melt the butter in a pan and sauté the leeks gently, stirring frequently, for about 5 minutes until they are soft but not brown.

2 Add the flour and cook for a further minute. Stir in the stock, wine, vinegar and honey, and bring to the boil. Simmer for 3 minutes.

3 To serve, add any pan juices from the roast meat, stir in the chopped fresh parsley and season.

Golden Potatoes

230 calories per serving

1.1 kg (2½ lb) old potatoes
salt and pepper
2 rosemary sprigs
6 cloves garlic (optional)
45 ml (3 tbsp) olive oil

1 Wash the potatoes and cut into large chunks, but do not peel. Place in cold, salted water, bring to the boil and simmer for 3 minutes. Drain. Strip the spiky rosemary leaves off the sprigs.

2 Place the potatoes in a roasting tin with the unskinned garlic cloves, rosemary and olive oil.

3 Roast at 200°C (400°F) mark 6 for 1½ hours, basting and turning a few times. Keep warm, uncovered.

Baked Tomato and Fennel

155 calories per serving

900 g (2 lb) Florence fennel bulbs, trimmed
900 g (2 lb) tomatoes, preferably beefsteak
75 ml (5 tbsp) white wine
45 ml (3 tbsp) chopped fresh thyme or 5 ml (1 tsp) dried
75 ml (5 tbsp) olive oil

1 Cut the fennel bulbs in halves or quarters, depending on size. Remove the core by making a 'V' in the base of the bulb, but make sure that the layers are held together. Quarter or halve the tomatoes.

2 Place the fennel in a roasting tin. Pour over the white wine and sprinkle over the thyme. Brush with olive oil.

3 Bake at 200°C (400°F) mark 6 for 45 minutes. Add the quartered or halved tomatoes, skin side up, and continue to cook for a further 30 minutes or until tender, basting twice during cooking time. Cover and keep warm.

Caramelized Apple Wafers

365 calories per serving

flour
450 g (1 lb) frozen puff pastry, thawed
beaten egg, to glaze
icing sugar
175 g (6 oz) white marzipan
2 small Granny Smith apples
25 g (1 oz) butter, melted
45 ml (3 tbsp) caster sugar

1 Draw a heart-shaped template 10 cm (4½in) across at its widest point and the same lengthways, and cut out. Draw a second heart-shaped template 2.5 cm (1 in) smaller all round; cut out.

2 On a lightly floured surface, thickly roll out the pastry to a 30.5 cm (12 in) square, and cut out six hearts, using the larger template. Place on a wetted baking sheet. Brush with beaten egg.

3 Dust icing sugar onto the work surface and roll out the marzipan to about a 5 mm (¼ in) thickness. Cut out six hearts, using the smaller template. Place on top of the pastry.

4 Peel, quarter and core the apples. Cut each quarter into three or four slices and arrange on the marzipan in a fan shape. Brush with melted butter and sprinkle over the caster sugar.

5 Bake at 220°C (425°F) mark 7 for about 15 minutes until the pastry is golden and the apples are beginning to caramelize. Serve warm, dusted with icing sugar.

Cinnamon Custard

220 calories per serving

450 ml (¾ pint) single cream
4 egg yolks
50 g (2 oz) caster sugar
2.5 ml (½ tsp) ground cinnamon

1 Slowly warm the cream in a saucepan. Gently beat the egg yolks and sugar together until they thicken and lighten in colour.

2 When the cream is hot but not boiling, pour it slowly onto the egg and sugar mixture, stirring constantly.

3 Pour the mixture back into a clean saucepan and cook the custard, stirring all the time, until it thickens and coats the back of a spoon. Do not boil the custard.

4 Stir in the cinnamon, then sieve the mixture to make a smooth custard. Place damp greaseproof paper on the surface to prevent a skin forming. Cool, then refrigerate until required.

Caramelized Apple Wafers

INSTANT SUCCESS ENTERTAINING

If you are cooking for friends after work, or simply want to spend as much time with your guests as possible, you will find the two following menus fail-safe and super-fast.

FIRST MENU

Papaya and Prawn Salad

Sweet Gingered Chicken

Yellow Split Peas with Coconut

Vanilla Ice with Espresso

Serves 6

SECOND MENU

Tomato, Pepper and Orange Soup

Hot Rosemary Ciabatta

Roast Salmon in Mustard Butter

Saffron Potatoes

Chilled Grapes and Vignotte

Serves 6

Sweet Gingered Chicken

(page 107)

First Menu

For a stylish, quick to prepare menu, look no further. Prawns coated in a chilli marinade, then served with exotic papaya, make a colourful tangy starter. Chinese-style chicken flavoured with fresh ginger is accompanied by creamy yellow split peas and coconut. A luxury ice cream with espresso coffee poured over makes a perfect finale.

Countdown

TO SERVE AT 8PM

7.15pm Preheat oven to 220°C (425°F) mark 7. Prepare Sweet Gingered Chicken and put in oven to cook. Put yellow split peas on to boil.

7.30pm Prepare Papaya and Prawn Salad.

8pm Serve salad. Keep chicken and split peas warm. Prepare Vanilla Ice and Espresso, when required.

ALTERNATIVE CATERING QUANTITIES

(Standard recipes serve 6)

Guests	25	50	100
Papaya and Prawn Salad	x 4	x 7	x 12
Sweet Gingered Chicken			
Chicken fillets	x 25	x 50	x 100
Apricot jam mix	x 4	x 8	x 16
Aubergines	x 4	x 8	x 16
Yellow Split Peas with Coconut	x 4	x 7	x 12
Vanilla Ice with Espresso			
Ice Cream	5 litres (9 pints)	9 litres (16 pints)	18 litres (32 pints)
Espresso Coffee	1.5 litres (2¾ pints)	3 litres (5¼ pints)	6 litres (10½ pints)

VITAL STATISTICS

Make sure you have plenty of oven space.

Papaya and Prawn Salad

For large quantities slice the papayas the day before, cover tightly and refrigerate. Make the dressing the day before and store in a cool place; add prawns just before serving. King prawns look the best but the smaller ones will go further. Grate the lemon rind for garnish, cover tightly and refrigerate for up to a day.

Sweet Gingered Chicken

You will need more than one oven when cooking this recipe for more than 25. Don't pack too much chicken into one tin or the pieces won't cook properly. Prepare the apricot mixture the day before, cover tightly and refrigerate. Slice the aubergine just before cooking.

Yellow Split Peas with Coconut

The peas absorb a lot of water so don't overcrowd the saucepans. A large domestic saucepan will only cope with 900 g (2 lb) split peas at a time. Grate the coconut the day before, cover tightly and store in a cool place.

Vanilla Ice with Espresso

Scoop the ice cream onto baking sheets lined with non-stick paper and return to the freezer; spoon into glasses at the last moment. Make coffee ahead and reheat gently to serve.

Papaya and Prawn Salad

Papaya and Prawn Salad

350 calories per serving

2 small red chillies
30 ml (2 tbsp) white wine vinegar
45-60 ml (3-4 tbsp) freshly squeezed lime juice (about 2 limes)
150 ml (¼ pint) olive oil
30 ml (2 tbsp) honey
salt and pepper
350 g (12 oz) cooked, peeled prawns
2-3 ripe papayas (see Cook's Tip)
grated lime rind, to garnish

1 Finely chop the chillies, discarding the seeds. Place in a blender or food processor with the vinegar, lime juice, olive oil, honey and seasoning. Blend until smooth. Stir in the prawns until coated.

2 Halve, then peel the papayas. Scoop out the black seeds and discard. Thinly slice the flesh and arrange on plates.

3 Carefully spoon the prawn mixture over the papaya slices. Serve immediately, garnished with grated lime rind.

COOK'S TIP

If the papayas are large you will find two are enough for six people.

Sweet Gingered Chicken

435 calories per serving

2.5 cm (1 in) piece fresh root ginger, peeled
120 ml (8 tbsp) apricot jam (about 1.75 g [6 oz])
75 ml (5 tbsp) light soy sauce
120 ml (8 tbsp) dry sherry
30 ml (2 tbsp) lemon juice
2 cloves garlic, skinned and crushed
350 g (12 oz) aubergine, thinly sliced
6 chicken breast fillets with skin, about 150 g (5 oz) each

1 Finely chop or grate the ginger. Mix together the jam, soy sauce, sherry and lemon juice. Add the garlic and ginger.

2 Line a large roasting tin with foil. Spread out the aubergine and chicken in the tin. Spoon the ginger mixture over.

3 Cook at 220°C (425°F) mark 7 for about 30-35 minutes, basting occasionally, until the chicken and aubergine are well browned and glazed. Add a little water, if necessary, towards the end of cooking.

Yellow Split Peas with Coconut

200 calories per serving

275 g (10 oz) yellow split peas
salt and pepper
75 g (3 oz) creamed coconut, grated
60 ml (4 tbsp) single cream (optional)
chopped fresh coriander, to garnish

1 Cook the split peas in boiling, salted water for 30-35 minutes or until just tender (there's no need to soak them first).

2 Drain the peas, return to the pan and stir in the coconut until melted throughout. Add the cream, if using; adjust seasoning. Serve garnished with coriander.

Vanilla Ice with Espresso

260 calories per serving

espresso coffee (see Cook's Tips)
vanilla or a 'nutty' luxury ice cream
chocolate-covered coffee beans or tiny chocolates, to accompany

1 Make up the espresso coffee according to the instructions on your machine.

2 Scoop ice cream into glasses and pour about 45-60 ml (3-4 tbsp) hot espresso over each serving.

3 Accompany the coffee vanilla ice cream with some chocolate-covered coffee beans.

COOK'S TIPS

If you don't have an espresso machine, use very strong black coffee or the sachets or jars of instant espresso coffee that can be found in most supermarkets.

Make sure you use a good, firm-textured, luxury ice cream made with real cream as the soft-scoop varieties melt too quickly and don't have the appropriate flavour.

Vanilla Ice with Espresso

Second Menu

For an impressive, yet instant meal, try this menu. Delicious Tomato, Pepper and Orange Soup, made using freshly squeezed orange juice, is served with popular ciabatta bread flavoured with rosemary and olive oil. Fresh salmon is lightly baked in a wholegrain mustard butter, making a perfect main course. Vignotte, a creamy, pasteurized cheese from the Champagne region of France, served with grapes, rounds off the menu.

Countdown

TO SERVE AT 8PM
7pm Make soup ready to reheat. Take cheese out of refrigerator.

7.30pm Preheat oven to 230°C (450°F) mark 8. Prepare salmon and put in oven to cook. Make Hot Rosemary Ciabatta and put in oven to heat. Prepare potatoes and put on to cook. Chill grapes.

7.45pm Reheat the soup to a simmer. Toss the salad leaves.

8pm Serve soup. Cover potatoes and salmon and keep warm.

VITAL STATISTICS
You will need plenty of oven space for this menu.

Tomato, Pepper and Orange Soup
If using stock cubes add only half the recommended amount to liquid as they can be very salty. Slice the oranges for garnish, cover and refrigerate for up to a day before using.

Hot Rosemary Ciabatta
It is best served really hot so cook in batches to bring out of the oven at the last moment.

Roast Salmon in Mustard Butter
For large quantities use individual pieces of salmon fillet, about 150g (5 oz) each. Spread out skin side up in large shallow ovenproof dishes and pour over the butter mixture. Cook at 230°C (450°F) mark 8 for about 12 minutes. Serve on salad leaves with mustard butter spooned over. Have all salad leaves washed, well drained and refrigerated in polythene bags ready for use.

Saffron Potatoes
Cook potatoes in smallish batches; if there are too many in a pan at one time they will break up when draining. They are delicious served cold too.

Chilled Grapes and Vignotte
Strip the grapes off their stalks and refrigerate ready to pour the wine over them at the last minute.

ALTERNATIVE CATERING QUANTITIES

(Standard recipes serve 6)

Guests	25	50	100
Tomato, Pepper and Orange Soup	x 4	x 7	x 12
Hot Rosemary Ciabatta	x 4	x 7	x 12
Roast Salmon in Mustard Butter			
125-175 g (4-6 oz)			
pieces salmon fillet with skin	x 25	x 50	x 100
Butter mixture	x 4	x 7	x 12
Salad leaves	900 g (2 lb)	1.6 kg (3½ lb)	2.7 kg (6 lb)
Saffron Potatoes	x 4	x 8	x 14
Chilled Grapes and Vignotte			
Grapes	2 kg (4½ lb)	3.6 kg (8 lb)	6.3 kg (14 lb)
Wine (if using)	900 ml (1½ pt)	1.4 l (2½ pt)	2.3 l (4 pt)
Vignotte	1.8 kg (4 lb)	3.2 kg (7 lb)	5.5 kg (12 lb)

Roast Salmon in Mustard Butter
Opposite: **Tomato, Pepper and Orange Soup**

Tomato, Pepper and Orange Soup

70 calories per serving

400 g (14 oz) can pimientos (red peppers), drained
a few rosemary sprigs or 5 ml (1 tsp) dried
10 ml (2 tsp) caster sugar
1 litre (1 ¾ pints) tomato juice
300 ml (½ pint) chicken stock
450 ml (¾ pint) freshly squeezed orange juice
salt and pepper
orange slices and rosemary sprigs, to garnish
Hot Rosemary Ciabatta, to serve

1 In a food processor, blend together the pimientos, rosemary, sugar and half the tomato juice.

2 Sieve the mixture into a saucepan and stir in the stock with the orange juice, remaining tomato juice and seasoning.

3 Bring to the boil and simmer gently for about 10 minutes. Adjust seasoning and serve, garnished.

Hot Rosemary Ciabatta

200 calories per serving

1 ready-to-bake ciabatta or French baguette
60 ml (4 tbsp) olive oil
few rosemary sprigs or 15 ml (1 tbsp) dried

1 Remove the bread from its packet. Cut in half lengthways, then into chunks. Place on foil.

2 Drizzle the oil and rosemary over. Wrap tightly. Cook at 230°C (450°F) mark 8 for 12-15 minutes.

Roast Salmon in Mustard Butter

560 calories per serving

1.1 kg (2½ lb) piece boned middle cut of salmon
175 g (6 oz) melted butter
45 ml (3 tbsp) wholegrain mustard
20 ml (4 tsp) dried dill weed
salt and pepper
275 g (10 oz) fresh spinach, rocket or mixed salad leaves

1 Open out the salmon like a book until almost flat by pressing along the backbone area. Place skin side up in a shallow ovenproof dish just large enough to hold it.

2 Mix together the butter, mustard, dill and seasoning. Pour over the salmon. Cook at 230°F (450°F) mark 8 for about 20 minutes or until just tender.

3 Toss the salad leaves and season well. Place on large plates.

4 Cut the salmon into thick slices and serve on top of the leaves with the mustard butter spooned over.

Saffron Potatoes

120 calories per serving

900 g (2 lb) old potatoes
salt and pepper
5 ml (1 tsp) saffron strands or 2 small sachets of ground saffron

1 Scrub the potatoes but do not peel. Cut the potatoes into thick slices.

2 Cook uncovered, in just enough boiling, salted water to cover, with the saffron, for 10 minutes or until almost tender. Increase the heat and bubble down the liquid until almost evaporated and the potatoes are tender (about 20 minutes cooking time in total). Drain, season and serve immediately.

Chilled Grapes and Vignotte

300 calories per serving
120 calories per serving grapes with wine

The simplest way to finish any meal is to offer chilled grapes with oatcakes and just one wonderful cheese, such as Vignotte, a creamy, pasteurized cheese from the Champagne region of France. It is available in some supermarkets and delicatessens; you will need at least 450 g (1 lb) for six — it vanishes quickly! If you feel your guests will be disappointed if there is no pudding, strip the grapes off their stalks and pour a chilled dessert wine such as Moscatel de Valencia over — 700 g (1½ lb) fruit will take 300 ml (½ pint) wine. Accompany with crème fraîche.

VEGETARIAN DINNER

Linger over the last hazy days of summer with an elegant vegetarian menu that makes the most of the season's abundant fresh produce.

Aubergine Timbales with Red Pepper Sauce

Mixed Mushroom Parcels

Grilled Artichoke Salad

Iced Orange and Lemon Terrine with Burnt Sugar Sauce

Serves 6

Aubergine Timbales with Red Pepper Sauce (page 113)

This healthy and stylish non-meat menu contains nutritious recipes using the best of foods in season. The Aubergine Timbales are filled with a ricotta cheese mixture and served with red pepper sauce. The Mixed Mushroom Parcels are made using filo pastry. To round off the meal, Iced Orange and Lemon Terrine is served with a burnt sugar sauce. Even meat-eaters will enjoy this fabulous dinner.

Countdown

UP TO 1 WEEK BEFORE
Make and freeze Iced Orange and Lemon Terrine.

THE DAY BEFORE
Prepare timbales to end of step 3, cover and refrigerate. Make Red Pepper Sauce to end of step 5. Refrigerate. Prepare mushroom filling, cover and refrigerate. Prepare French Dressing, cover and refrigerate. Wash and quarter lettuces. Place in plastic bag and refrigerate. Grill artichoke hearts. Cool, cover and refrigerate. Make Burnt Sugar Sauce, cover and refrigerate.

TO SERVE AT 8PM
6pm Complete mushroom parcels, cover loosely with cling film and refrigerate.

7pm Preheat oven to 190°C (375°F) mark 5. Remove salad dressing and artichoke hearts from refrigerator.

7.30pm Put timbales in oven. Slice terrine, place on a baking sheet lined with greaseproof paper; return to freezer until required.

7.45pm Reheat Red Pepper Sauce and add basil. Place mushroom parcels on a hot baking sheet and cook.

8pm Serve starter.

FREEZER NOTES

Make Red Pepper Sauce to end of step 5. Freeze. Thaw overnight at cool room temperature. Make and freeze Iced Orange and Lemon Terrine. Serve from freezer. Make and freeze Burnt Sugar Sauce. Thaw overnight in refrigerator.

ALTERNATIVE CATERING QUANTITIES

(Standard recipes serve 6)

Guests	25	50	100
Aubergine Timbales			
with Red Pepper Sauce	x 4	x 8	x 16
Mixed Mushroom Parcels	x 4	x 7	x 12
Grilled Artichoke Salad	x 4	x 8	x 16
Iced Orange and Lemon Terrine			
with Burnt Sugar Sauce	x 3	x 6	x 12
Mandarins/Oranges for			
segments (no. of fruit)	12	24	48

VITAL STATISTICS

You will need plenty of oven space for this menu.

Aubergine Timbales

Divide the mixture between 25/50/100 ramekins respectively. Alternatively, don't blend the cheese filling but simply beat ingredients together; spoon a little onto each grilled aubergine slice. Roll up, grilled side out, and place seam side down on lightly oiled baking sheets. You will have about twenty rolls. Bake at 190°C (375°F) mark 5 for about 15 minutes. Serve with the Red Pepper Sauce.

Mixed Mushroom Parcels

Allow plenty of time to make these filo parcels. First cut all the pastry into squares and then stack them into small piles. Wrap each pile in cling film until ready to use as filo pastry dries and cracks when exposed to air and becomes hard to handle. These parcels freeze very well or can be prepared up to 24 hours ahead; cover loosely and refrigerate.

Iced Orange and Lemon Terrine with Burnt Sugar Sauce

Prepare and freeze in double quantities only; no more or the mixture may separate out. Once firm ease out of the tins, overwrap and return to the freezer so that the tins can be used again. Slice well ahead; place on baking sheets lined with greaseproof paper and return to the freezer until required.

Aubergine Timbales with Red Pepper Sauce

500 calories per serving

2 aubergines, about 275 g (10 oz) each (preferably short, fat shapes)

90 ml (6 tbsp) olive oil

450 g (1 lb) ricotta cheese

175 g (6 oz) freshly grated Parmesan cheese

4 egg yolks

5 ml (1 tsp) freshly grated nutmeg

salt and pepper

small handful fresh basil

2 large red peppers, about 225 g (8 oz) each

4 tomatoes, about 350 g (12 oz) total weight

2 cloves garlic, skinned and crushed

30 ml (2 tbsp) passata or 15 ml (1 tbsp) tomato paste

45 ml (3 tbsp) pesto sauce

1 Finely slice the aubergines lengthways. Place on an oiled baking sheet and brush lightly with olive oil. Grill one side until well browned. Set aside.

2 To make the filling, place the ricotta and Parmesan cheeses, egg yolks, nutmeg and seasoning in a food processor and blend until smooth. Tear the basil. Reserve 15 ml (1 tbsp) and add the rest to the mixture.

3 Line six 150-175 ml (5-6 fl oz) dariole moulds or ramekins with the aubergine slices, overlapping them with the browned sides facing outwards. Leave a long edge hanging over the outside. Fill each mould with the cheese mixture, pushing it down firmly. Fold the edges of aubergine over the top of the filling to enclose.

4 Place on a baking sheet. Cook at 190°C (375°F) mark 5 for about 15 minutes or until firm.

5 Meanwhile, make the Red Pepper Sauce. Seed and roughly chop the red peppers and tomatoes. Place in a saucepan with the garlic, passata and 60 ml (4 tbsp) water. Season well. Cover and cook over a gentle heat for 10 minutes. Blend in a blender until smooth and pass through a nylon sieve.

6 Stir in the remaining basil and gently reheat the sauce. To serve, place a pool of sauce on six small plates. Unmould the timbales and place in the centre. Drizzle a little pesto around each timbale.

Mixed Mushroom Parcels

450 calories per serving

50 g (2 oz) wild or brown rice

175 g (6 oz) each onion, carrot and celery

700 g (1½ lb) brown and white cap mushrooms, mixed

75 g (3 oz) no-soak dried apricots

75 g (3 oz) hazelnuts, toasted

butter

2 cloves garlic, skinned and crushed

225 g (8 oz) jar mixed wild mushrooms (see Cook's Tip)

salt and pepper

about 600 g (1¼ lb) filo pastry

15 ml (1 tbsp) sesame seeds

60 ml (4 tbsp) chopped fresh chives

200 g (7 oz) crème fraîche

chives, to garnish

1 Cook the rice in plenty of boiling, salted water until tender. Drain and set aside. Chop the onion, carrot, celery and fresh mushrooms. Chop the apricots and nuts.

2 Melt 25 g (1 oz) butter in a large frying pan and cook the onion and garlic for about 10 minutes or until soft and brown. Add the celery and carrot and fry for 3-4 minutes.

3 Add a further 25 g (1 oz) butter and the chopped fresh mushrooms to the vegetables. Cook uncovered, stirring, until all excess moisture has evaporated and the mixture is quite dry (about 15 minutes). Add the drained wild mushrooms and cook for a further 5 minutes. Remove from the heat and set aside. Season.

4 Stir the nuts, wild rice and apricots into the mushroom mixture.

5 Cut the pastry into about forty 18-20.5 cm (7-8 in) squares (see Cook's Tip). Divide into two or three stacks and wrap in cling film while preparing the parcels. Butter one square of pastry, top with a second piece of pastry and butter again. Spoon about one-twentieth of the mushroom mixture into the centre and gather up the sides to form a parcel. Press gently to seal. Continue with the remaining pastry and mushroom mixture. Brush with melted butter and sprinkle with sesame seeds.

6 Place the parcels on a heated baking sheet. Cook at 190°C (375°F) mark 5 for 25-30 minutes.

7 Stir the chives into the crème fraîche; season. Arrange the parcels on plates with a spoonful of the sauce. Garnish with chives, snipped on the diagonal, if wished. Serve the remaining sauce separately.

COOK'S TIPS

Most supermarkets stock jars of mixed wild mushrooms in oil. Filo pastry sheets come in a variety of sizes. Cut squares to waste as little pastry as possible and prepare slightly more or fewer parcels as necessary.

Grilled Artichoke Salad

60 calories per serving

Drain a 400 g (14 oz) can artichoke hearts. Halve, season and brush with olive oil, then grill until charred. Quarter three Little Gem lettuces and toss in French Dressing with the artichokes.

Iced Orange and Lemon Terrine with Burnt Sugar Sauce

375 calories per serving

4 egg yolks (see note)
30 ml (2 tbsp) caster sugar
300 ml (½ pint) whipping cream
finely grated rind and juice of 1 large orange
finely grated rind and juice of 1 lemon
125 g (4 oz) caster sugar
juice of ½ lemon
pinch of salt
150 ml (¼ pint) single cream
mandarin or orange segments, to decorate

1 Using an electric whisk, whisk together the egg yolks and sugar for 5 minutes or until pale and thick.

2 Lightly whip the cream until it just holds its shape. Fold into the egg mixture, along with the orange juice and orange and lemon rind. The mixture will become quite liquid.

3 Line a 1.1 litre (2 pint) terrine or loaf tin with cling film. Pour in the mixture. Freeze for 3 hours or overnight.

4 To make the sauce, put the sugar, plus 125 ml (4 fl oz) water and the lemon juice in a heavy-based saucepan. Place over a medium heat for about 3 minutes until the sugar has dissolved. Do not stir. Increase the heat and cook for about 5 minutes until the sugar is a light caramel colour. Add the salt and, off the heat, stir in the cream. Chill for 3 hours or overnight.

5 Briefly dip the tin in hot water, then invert the terrine on to a serving plate. Remove the cling film and slice with a hot knife. Soften at room temperature for about 10 minutes. Serve with the Burnt Sugar Sauce and decorate with mandarin segments.

NOTE

The young, the elderly, pregnant women and people with immune-deficiency diseases should not eat raw eggs, due to the possible risk of salmonella.

Left: **Mixed Mushroom Parcels** (page 113)
Right: **Iced Orange and Lemon Terrine with Burnt Sugar Sauce**

SUMMER LUNCH

Simple summer flavours can create the tastiest of menus. Colourful and light, these recipes are perfect to enjoy with friends.

King Prawn Filos

Mediterranean Roast Chicken

Pepper Sauce

Golden Vegetables

Mixed Herb Salad

Red Fruit Mallow

Serves 6

The exciting starter of King Prawn Filos is served with Mango Sauce and Thai Sweet Chilli Sauce for dipping. Mediterranean Roast Chicken follows — chicken breasts filled with a spinach, basil, tomato, ricotta cheese and pinenut stuffing. This dish can also be served cold with salads.

A meringue topping is piped on to summer berries for a fitting finale to a glorious summer meal.

Countdown

THE DAY BEFORE
Make Pepper Sauce; cool, cover and refrigerate. Complete chicken recipe to end of step 3. Make salad dressing; cover and store in a cool place. Follow step 3 only of King Prawn Filos; keep refrigerated.

IN THE MORNING
Dice sweet potatoes and summer squash. Cover with cold water. Wash, dry and refrigerate salad leaves in polythene bags. Follow steps 1-2 of King Prawn Filos. Prepare Red Fruit Mallow to the end of step 4; set aside in a cool place but not in refrigerator, ready to cook later.

TO SERVE AT 1PM
12 noon Preheat oven.

12.20pm Complete step 1 of Golden Vegetables. Heat oil, then put vegetables in oven. Put chicken in to roast.

12.30pm Heat oil for prawns. Arrange leaves for prawns on plates.

12.45pm Cook King Prawn Filos. Gently reheat Pepper Sauce.

12.55pm Toss salad with dressing. Put Golden Vegetables into a serving dish and keep warm. Keep chicken warm in a low oven.

1pm Serve King Prawn Filos. Reduce oven temperature to 180°C (350°F) mark 4.

1.15pm Put Red Fruit Mallows into oven to cook.

VITAL STATISTICS

Make sure you have plenty of oven space available for this menu.

King Prawn Filos
For large quantities we advise frying these ahead then reheating them, see Cook's Tips.

Mediterranean Roast Chicken
These can be served hot or cold. If serving hot, don't overcrowd the roasting tins or the chicken won't cook through. Pour in just enough stock to moisten the chicken without drowning it. If serving cold, provide lots of crusty bread and bulk up the salad quantities to replace the Golden Vegetables.

Golden Vegetables
Spread these out in roasting tins so that they have room to brown.

Red Fruit Mallow
It may sound daring to serve hot desserts for a large crowd but these can be prepared well ahead ready to bake at the last minute (see Cook's Tips). Divide the mixture between 25/50/100 ramekins respectively or spoon each quantity of the apple mixture into a 1.1 litre (2 pint) shallow ovenproof dish. Top with meringue and then bake as before.

ALTERNATIVE CATERING QUANTITIES

(Standard recipes serve 6)

Guests	25	50	100
King Prawn Filos	x 4	x 7	x 12
Mediterranean Roast Chicken			
Chicken supremes	25	50	100
remaining ingredients	x 4	x 8	x 16
Pepper Sauce	x 4	x 7	x 14
Golden Vegetables	x 4	x 7	x 13
Mixed Herb Salad	x 3	x 6	x 12
Red Fruit Mallow	x 4	x 8	x 16

FREEZER NOTES

Prepare Pepper Sauce; cool, cover and freeze. To use, thaw overnight at cool room temperature then reheat to serve. Open freeze King Prawn Filos at end of step 2; pack once they are frozen. To use, fry from frozen for 2-3 minutes. (Do not re-freeze previously frozen prawns.)

King Prawn Filos

King Prawn Filos

315 calories per serving

18 large, cooked king prawns, about 225 g (8 oz) total weight (see Cook's Tips)

1 large bunch coriander, about 50 g (2 oz)

salt and pepper

about 175 g (6 oz) filo pastry

2 egg yolks, beaten

1 large ripe mango

45 ml (3 tbsp) mayonnaise

juice of 1 lime

about 60 ml (4 tbsp) bought Thai Sweet Chilli Sauce, for dipping

oil, for deep frying

banana leaves (see Cook's Tips) or mixed salad leaves, to garnish

1 Shell the prawns if necessary. Roughly chop the coriander and set aside 15 ml (1 tbsp). Mix the remainder with the prawns and season. Cut the filo pastry into thirty-six 10 cm (4 in) squares. Cover with cling film to prevent drying out.

2 Layer two squares of pastry directly on top of each other, brushing lightly with egg yolk between the layers and again on the top. Place a prawn in the centre and roll it up diagonally, pressing well to seal. Wrap and seal the remaining prawns in the same way. Chill on a wire rack (they tend to become soggy on a baking sheet) until ready to cook – do not cover.

3 Peel and remove the flesh from the mango. Blend the flesh, mayonnaise and lime juice in a food processor until smooth; season. Add the reserved coriander to chilli sauce. Put the mango sauce and chilli sauce into two small bowls. Cover and refrigerate.

4 Heat oil in a deep-fat fryer or a large saucepan to 165°-175°C (330°- 345°F) or until a piece of bread frizzles gently in the oil. Fry the prawn filos in batches for about 2 minutes or until golden and crisp. Drain on absorbent kitchen paper, then keep warm, uncovered, in a low oven until ready to serve.

5 Serve the prawns on banana leaves or mixed salad leaves with the mango sauce and Thai Sweet Chilli Sauce for dipping.

COOK'S TIPS

These pastries are best when fried at the last moment, though they are still delicious if fried ahead and reheated. Place on a baking sheet, loosely cover with foil, and reheat at 200°C (400°F) mark 6 for 10-12 minutes.

If you can't find large king prawns, use smaller ones and place two inside each parcel; 36 of the smaller prawns will weigh about 225 g (8 oz) too.

Banana leaves are available from oriental supermarkets.

Mediterranean Roast Chicken

350 calories per serving

15 g (¼ oz) fresh basil

50 g (2 oz) sun-dried tomatoes in oil, drained

450 g (1 lb) fresh spinach or 225 g (8 oz) frozen leaf spinach, thawed

salt and pepper

grated nutmeg

175 g (6 oz) ricotta cheese

1 egg yolk

25 g (1 oz) pinenuts, toasted

six 125 g (4 oz) chicken breast supremes with skin

olive oil

150 ml (¼ pint) chicken stock

Pepper Sauce, to accompany

fresh herbs, to garnish

1 Shred the basil and reserve the stalks for the Pepper Sauce. Finely chop the sun-dried tomatoes.

2 Wash the fresh spinach, then shred roughly (see Cook's Tips). Place in a large saucepan with no extra water, cover and cook over gentle heat for about 3-4 minutes or until wilted. Drain and squeeze out any moisture. Season with salt, pepper and a little nutmeg to taste; cool. Mix the spinach with the sundried tomatoes, basil, ricotta cheese, egg yolk and pinenuts.

3 Ease up the skin on the chicken supremes to form a pocket and push the stuffing underneath. Tie with fine string; cover and chill for about 2 hours.

4 Put the chicken into a roasting tin and brush lightly with olive oil. Season and pour in the chicken stock. Cook at 200°C (400°F) mark 6 for 35-40 minutes or until the chicken is tender, basting occasionally with the stock.

5 To serve, lift out of the cooking juices. Cut two or three slices from each fillet to reveal the stuffing. Place on a pool of Pepper Sauce and garnish with fresh herbs. Alternatively, serve sliced cold with salads.

COOK'S TIPS

For a change, make double quantity of stuffing mixture and spoon into three boned poussins. Secure with wooden satay sticks or string. Cook as before for about 50 minutes. Allow to sit for 5 minutes before removing sticks or string. Thickly slice to serve.

If using frozen spinach, use frozen leaf not chopped. Simply drain well and chop — there is no need to cook. (Readychopped frozen spinach is too watery.)

Pepper Sauce

120 calories per serving

45 ml (3 tbsp) olive oil
4 red peppers, seeded and roughly chopped
5 shallots or 1 medium onion, skinned and finely sliced
5 cloves garlic, skinned
1 star anise (see Cook's Tips)
150 ml (¼ pint) white wine
450 ml (¾ pint) vegetable stock
2 fresh basil stalks (from the Mediterranean Roast Chicken)
salt and pepper

1 Heat the oil in a saucepan and cook the peppers, shallots, garlic and star anise, covered, over a low heat, without browning, for about 10 minutes.

2 Add the wine, stock, basil and seasoning; cover and simmer for a further 20 minutes or until the vegetables are quite tender.

3 Cool slightly, remove the star anise and blend in a food processor until smooth. Sieve and keep warm over a gentle heat.

COOK'S TIPS

Star anise is a star-shaped spice that tastes strongly of aniseed, available from the spice racks in major supermarkets. However, the sauce still tastes good without it.

This sauce freezes extremely well. When red peppers are at their cheapest make a large batch of Pepper Sauce.

Golden Vegetables

180 calories per serving

900 g (2 lb) mixed sweet potatoes and summer squash
salt and pepper
60 ml (4 tbsp) olive oil

1 Scrub the potatoes. Cut the vegetables into 2.5 cm (1 in) cubes. Cook in boiling, salted water for 2 minutes, then drain well.

2 Meanwhile, place the oil in a roasting tin and heat at 200°C (400°F) mark 6 for 2-3 minutes or until hot.

3 Add the vegetables and cook on the top shelf for about 30-40 minutes or until golden brown, stirring occasionally, season well.

Mixed Herb Salad

115 calories per serving

2 bunches watercress
50 g (2 oz) mâche or lamb's lettuce
50 g (2 oz) rocket
30 ml (2 tbsp) sherry vinegar
15 ml (1 tbsp) wholegrain mustard
15 ml (1 tbsp) light soft brown sugar
60 ml (4 tbsp) olive oil
salt and pepper
50 g (2 oz) blanched broad beans
handful of mixed fresh herb sprigs

1 Wash and dry all the salad leaves. Whisk together the vinegar, mustard, sugar, oil and seasoning.

2 Just before serving toss the salad ingredients and the broad beans into the dressing with the herb sprigs.

Red Fruit Mallow

195 calories per serving

450 g (1 lb) Bramley cooking apples or 350 g (12 oz) can or jar stewed apples with no added sugar
15 ml (1 tbsp) light soft brown sugar
225 g (8 oz) mixed berries, such as sliced strawberries, blackberries, redcurrants
3 egg whites
175 g (6 oz) caster sugar
25 g (1 oz) skinned hazelnuts, roughly chopped

1 Peel and roughly chop the apples, then place in a saucepan with the brown sugar and 15 ml (1 tbsp) water. Cook, stirring, over a gentle heat until the apples have become soft but not too pulpy. Cool. (If using ready-stewed apple, sweeten to taste but do not cook.)

2 Mix the berries with the apple and divide evenly among six 150 ml (¼ pint) ramekins or individual ovenproof dishes.

3 Whisk the egg whites until they just stand in soft peaks, then gradually whisk in the caster sugar, adding about 15 ml (1 tbsp) at a time until all the sugar has been added. The mixture should look thick and shiny.

4 Fill a piping bag fitted with a 2.5 cm (1 in) plain nozzle with the meringue mixture and pipe in circles on top of the fruit to form a pyramid, or spoon the meringue over the fruit in a tall mound. Sprinkle with the hazelnuts.

5 Bake at 180°C (350°F) mark 4 for 20-25 minutes or until risen and lightly golden. Serve with thick Jersey cream.

Red Fruit Mallow

AUTUMN FEAST

This perfect menu for an autumn party has a distinctly French feel.

Pumpkin and Tomato Soup

Fillet of Beef with Roquefort and Chestnuts

Lentils with Shallots

Prune and Armagnac Ice Cream

Serves 6

This autumn menu has a definite French flavour, ideal to serve to remember time spent on holiday in France. The highlight is the fillet of beef served with chestnuts and a rich Roquefort sauce. For the dessert, the prunes need to be steeped in Armagnac preferably two to three weeks before making the ice cream.

Countdown

TWO TO THREE WEEKS BEFORE
Prepare Prunes in Armagnac.

ONE WEEK BEFORE
Make and freeze ice cream.

THE DAY BEFORE
Make Pumpkin and Tomato Soup; cool, cover and refrigerate. Skin shallots and refrigerate in polythene bags. Mix cheese and Stilton; cover and chill. Grill chestnuts.

TO SERVE AT 1PM
11.30am Follow step 4 of Fillet of Beef, set aside.

12 noon Preheat oven to 220°C (425°F) mark 7.

12.15pm Brown beef, calculate cooking time and put in oven to roast.

12.20pm Put shallots in a roasting tin with a little oil and seasoning. Roast for about 30 minutes, turning occasionally. Put lentils on to boil.

12.30pm Place ice cream in refrigerator.

12.45pm Reheat soup. Drain lentils, cover and keep warm. Mix with shallots just before serving. Reheat sauce for beef and whisk in Roquefort butter; keep warm.

1pm Serve soup. Keep beef warm in very low oven.

FREEZER NOTES

Pack and freeze the soup at the end of step 3. Thaw overnight at cool room temperature; complete as directed.

ALTERNATIVE CATERING QUANTITIES

(Standard recipes serve 6)

Guests	25	50	100
Pumpkin and Tomato Soup	x 3	x 6	x 10
Fillet of Beef with	x 4	x 7	x 13
Roquefort and Chestnuts			
Lentils	900 g	1.6 kg	2.7 kg
	(2 lb)	(3½ lb)	(6 lb)
Shallots/button onions	1.4 kg	2.7 kg	4.5 kg
	(3 lb)	(6 lb)	(10 lb)
Prune and Armagnac Ice Cream	x 4	x 7	x 13
Prunes in Armagnac	x 1½	x 3	x 5

VITAL STATISTICS

Fillet of Beef with Roquefort and Chestnuts
It is best to cook several 900 g (2 lb) fillets of beef rather than larger ones where the timing can be more difficult. Cook in rotation to allow a few minutes carving time before the next piece is ready. Slice fairly thinly and serve out to your guests so that you can monitor portion control! Prepare the sauce base (see step 4) ahead of time ready to reheat and add the Roquefort butter at serving time. Grill the chestnuts the day before; store in a cool place.

Prune and Armagnac Ice Cream
Well ahead of time, scoop onto baking sheets, lined with greaseproof paper and return to the freezer until ready to serve.

Fillet of Beef with Roquefort and Chestnuts

Pumpkin and Tomato Soup

115 calories per serving

900 g (2 lb) pumpkin
45 ml (3 tbsp) olive oil
225 g (8 oz) onion, skinned and chopped
3 sticks celery, chopped
450 g (1 lb) tomatoes, chopped
1.6 litres (2 ¾ pints) vegetable stock
30 ml (2 tbsp) tomato paste
few sprigs thyme
salt and pepper
chopped fresh herbs, to garnish

1 Cut the pumpkin into thin slices, discarding the coarse skin and seeds. Heat the oil in a saucepan and cook the onion and celery for about 5 minutes. Add the pumpkin and tomatoes and cook for 1-2 minutes.

2 Stir in the stock, tomato paste, thyme and seasoning. Bring to the boil, cover and simmer for 40 minutes or until tender.

3 Cool the soup slightly, remove the herbs, then blend until smooth. Sieve. Reheat the soup. Season and garnish.

Fillet of Beef with Roquefort and Chestnuts

500 calories per serving

75 g (3 oz) Roquefort cheese
75 g (3 oz) unsalted butter, softened
900 g (2 lb) fillet of beef
30 ml (2 tbsp) olive oil
50 g (2 oz) onion, skinned and chopped
75 ml (5 tbsp) port
300 ml (½ pint) beef stock
salt and pepper
439 g (15.5 oz) can whole chestnuts in water, drained
45 ml (3 tbsp) chopped fresh parsley
flat-leaf parsley, to garnish
lentils with baked shallots or button onions, to accompany (see Countdown)

1 Crumble the cheese and beat with the butter. Cover and chill.

2 Tie the beef with fine string. Heat the olive oil in a frying pan, preferably non-stick and brown the beef well. Place on a wire rack standing over a roasting tin.

3 Roast at 220°C (425°F) mark 7 for 30 minutes for rare, 35 minutes for medium rare and 40 minutes for well done beef.

4 Meanwhile, discard the fat from the frying pan. Add the onion, port and stock to the pan and boil until reduced by about a half.

5 Over a low heat, whisk in Roquefort butter until smooth. Adjust seasoning and keep warm.

6 Grill chestnuts for a few minutes until browned. Mix with the parsley.

7 Slice the beef to serve. Garnish with the chestnuts. Serve with the Roquefort sauce and a simple accompaniment, such as simmered green lentils tossed with baked shallots or button onions (see Countdown) and a Shredded Red Salad (see page 42).

Prune and Armagnac Ice Cream

290 calories per serving

6 egg yolks
150 g (5 oz) caster sugar
600 ml (1 pint) milk
150 ml (5 fl oz) double cream
50 ml (2 fl oz) syrup from Prunes in Armagnac
250 g (9 oz) Prunes in Armagnac, drained weight (see page 126)

1 Beat the egg yolks and sugar until thick and pale. Bring the milk to almost boiling and pour on to the egg, stirring well. Return to the pan and cook gently, stirring, until the custard thickens slightly — do not boil. Cool.

2 Lightly whip the cream. Stir into the custard with the syrup from the Prunes in Armagnac.

3 Pour the mixture into a shallow freezer container. Cover and freeze until mushy — about 4 hours. Meanwhile stone, if necessary, and chop the prunes.

4 Take the mushy ice cream from the freezer and beat to break down the ice crystals. Stir in the prunes and freeze again until firm.

5 Place the ice cream in the refrigerator for about 1½ hours before serving.

COOK'S TIP

In Gascony you can buy every kind of fruit preserved in Armagnac – prunes are a favourite. It is best to leave the prunes for three weeks to absorb the delicious Armagnac juices.

Prunes in Armagnac

148 calories per serving

450 g (1 lb) large prunes
about 900 ml (1½ pints) tea
125 g (4 oz) granulated sugar
about 300 ml (½ pint) Armagnac

1 Cover the prunes with tea and simmer for 5 minutes. Cool, cover and soak overnight.

2 Next day, dissolve the sugar in 125 ml (4 fl oz) water. Bring to the boil, boil for 2 minutes, then pour into a bowl and leave to cool.

3 Drain the prunes. Place in a clean 1.1 litre (2 pint) jar. Pour the syrup over and top with Armagnac.

4 Tightly cover the jar and store in the refrigerator. They will keep for a year or more.

Prune and Armagnac Ice Cream (page 125)

Quantity Chart

Here are approximate quantities to serve 12 people, but refer to individual menus for more specific information. For 25 people, multiply the quantities by two. For 50 people multiply by four. For 75 people multiply by five and a half. For 100 people multiply by seven.

Salads
Tomato — allow 700 g (1½ lb)
Salad leaves — allow 2 medium heads
Cucumber — allow 1 large

Dressings
French Dressing (see page 128) allow 175 ml (6 fl oz)
Mayonnaise — allow 300 ml (½ pint)

Bread
Fresh bread — allow 1 large loaf
Medium sliced bread — allow 1 large loaf (about 24 slices)

Cheeses
For a wine and cheese party — allow 1.4 kg (3 lb)
To serve at the end of a meal — allow 700 g (1½ lb)

Butter
To serve with bread or biscuits and cheese — allow 225 g (8 oz)
To serve with bread and biscuits and cheese — allow 350 g (12 oz)

Cream
For pudding or dessert — allow 600 ml (1 pint) single cream for 15-20
For coffee — allow 300 ml (½ pint) single cream for 12-15

Milk
Allow 450 ml (¾ pint) for 12 cups tea

Coffee
Ground coffee — allow about 125 g (4 oz) for 12 medium cups
Instant — allow about 75 g (3 oz) for 12 large cups

Tea
Allow about 25 g (1 oz) for 12 medium cups

Basic Recipes

FRENCH DRESSING

95 calories per serving
Makes about 175 ml (6 fl oz)
Serves about 12

---

125 ml (4 fl oz) oil - half olive, half sunflower

45 ml (3 tbsp) vinegar or lemon juice

salt and pepper

5 ml (1 tsp) caster sugar

1 large clove garlic, skinned and crushed
(optional)

5 ml (1 tsp) Dijon mustard

---

1 Place all the ingredients in a screw top
jar and shake well to mix.
2 Store in a cool place for up to two
weeks. Shake well before using.

COOK'S TIP

For special occasions, add a little walnut
or hazelnut oil to the dressing in place of
some of the sunflower oil.
Not suitable for freezing

COLESLAW

230 calories per serving Serves 12

---

1 small white cabbage, about 550 g (1¼lb)
total weight

450 g (1 lb) carrots, peeled

175 g (6 oz) onion, skinned

6 sticks of celery

90 ml (6 tbsp) chopped fresh parsley

75 g (3 oz) raisins

300 ml (½ pint) mayonnaise

30 ml (2 tbsp) wholegrain mustard

45 ml (3 tbsp) lemon juice

salt and pepper

watercress sprigs, to garnish (optional)

---

1 Finely shred the cabbage, discarding
any coarse outer leaves. Coarsely grate
the carrots and finely slice the onion and
celery.
2 In a large bowl mix all the ingredients
together, stirring well. Cover and chill for
at least 3 hours before serving. Stir well
before serving and garnish with watercress, if wished.
Not suitable for freezing

RICE SALAD

185 calories per serving Serves 12

---

275 g (10 oz) long-grain white rice or long-
grain and wild rice mixed

salt and pepper

275 g (10 oz) frozen mixed diced vegetables

4 sticks celery

2 dessert apples

60 ml (4 tbsp) chopped fresh parsley

90 ml (6 tbsp) French Dressing

50 g (2 oz) raisins

50 g (2 oz) salted peanuts

---

1 Cook the rice in a pan of boiling salted
water until tender. Drain in a colander,
rinsing under cold water to stop it cooking further. Drain again. Cook the mixed
vegetables until tender. Drain.
2 Roughly chop the celery. Quarter, core
and roughly chop the apples.
3 Mix all the ingredients together, seasoning well. Cover and refrigerate until
required.

COOK'S TIP

The rice salad can be made without the
apple up to two days ahead. Cover and
refrigerate, adding the apple on the day
and stirring well to mix.
Not suitable for freezing

MIXED BEAN SALAD

170 calories per serving Serves 12

---

three 425 g (15 oz) cans beans
(see Cook's Tip)

1 cucumber

salt and pepper

700 g (1½ lb) tomatoes

2 bunches spring onions, trimmed

chopped fresh parsley or coriander

125 ml (4 fl oz) French Dressing

---

1 Drain the beans and rinse under cold
water. Drain again.
2 Roughly dice the cucumber, sprinkle
with salt and leave to stand for 30 minutes. Rinse under cold running water and
leave to drain. Dry on absorbent kitchen
paper.
3 Roughly chop the tomatoes and finely

chop the spring onions, discarding any
dark leaves.
4 Mix all the ingredients together, adding
herbs to taste. Cover and refrigerate until
required. Stir well before serving.

COOK'S TIP

Use a mix of canned beans or peas, per-
haps red kidney, cannellini and chick
peas, choosing them for a good colour
combination. This salad can be made up
to two days ahead.
Not suitable for freezing

POTATO SALAD

255 calories per serving Serves 12

1.8 kg (4 lb) even-sized old potatoes

salt and pepper

1 large bunch spring onions, trimmed

150 ml (¼ pint) mayonnaise

150 ml (5 fl oz) soured cream

150 ml (5 fl oz) single cream

lemon juice, to taste

1 clove garlic, skinned and crushed
(optional)

paprika, to garnish

---

1 Scrub the potatoes, then cook in a pan
of boiling salted water until tender. Drain.
When quite cold, peel and cut into
chunks. Chop the spring onions, reserving a few tops for garnish.
2 In a large bowl, mix together the mayonnaise, soured cream, single cream,
lemon juice to taste, garlic and seasoning. Add the potatoes and onions and stir
gently to mix.
3 Pile the salad into a serving dish and
garnish with the reserved onion tops and
a sprinkling of paprika.

VARIATIONS

● Add chopped celery and green pepper
to the salad and a dash of chilli powder
to the mayonnaise.
● Use small new potatoes, leaving their
skins on to serve.
● Replace the single cream with natural
yogurt for a sharper dressing.
● If preferred serve the cooked new
potatoes warm with French Dressing and
a few chopped spring onions.
Not suitable for freezing

Freeze Ahead or Prepare Ahead Recipes

SMOKED SALMON AND PEPPERCORN ROLL

130 calories per serving Serves 8

For 25 people, multiply the quantity by three; for 50 multiply by five; and for 100 multiply by ten.

10 ml (2 tsp) pink peppercorns (in brine)
225 g (8 oz) thin slices of smoked salmon, not previously frozen
225 g (8 oz) full-fat soft cheese
125 g (4 oz) unsalted butter, softened
30 ml (2 tbsp) lemon juice
60 ml (4 tbsp) single cream
mixed salad leaves, to serve
Hot Lemon Bread, to accompany

1 Finely chop the pink peppercorns and two slices of smoked salmon, about 50 g (2 oz). Beat together the soft cheese, butter, lemon juice and cream. Beat in the peppercorns and smoked salmon. Chill for about 40 minutes.

2 On greaseproof paper, lay out the remaining smoked salmon, overlapping to form a rectangle 25.5 x 10 cm (10 x 4 in).

3 With wet hands, shape the cheese mixture into a roll about 25.5 cm (10 in) long and place in the centre of the smoked salmon, smoothing it off with a spoon. Fold the salmon edges around the cheese to enclose and roll tightly in the greaseproof paper. Place in the freezer for about 1½ hours.

4 Cut the roll into thick slices. Arrange on a bed of salad leaves. Cover with cling film and thaw in the refrigerator for about 2 hours. Serve as a starter with Hot Lemon Bread.

To Freeze: Freeze at end of step 3.
To Use: Thaw roll for ¾-1 hour at room temperature. Slice, thaw in refrigerator for about 5 hours.

HOT LEMON BREAD

300 calories per serving Serves 8

For 25 people, multiply the quantity by three; for 50 multiply by five; and for 100 multiply by ten.

125 g (4 oz) butter, softened
grated rind and juice of 1 lemon
freshly ground black pepper
1 large 'nutty-textured' loaf

1 Beat together the butter, grated lemon rind, 30 ml (2 tbsp) lemon juice, and plenty of freshly ground black pepper. Mix these ingredients together well.

2 Cut the loaf into 2.5 cm (1 in) slices. Halve each slice. Liberally spread both sides of the bread with the lemon butter.

3 Reshape the loaf. Spread any remaining butter over the top of the bread and wrap the whole loaf completely in foil.

4 Bake at 200°C (400°F) mark 6 for 20-25 minutes. Open out the foil for the last 5 minutes. Serve hot.

To Freeze: Pack and freeze the bread at the end of step 3.
To Use: Thaw overnight at cool room temperature. Bake as above, opening out foil for last 5 minutes.

MIXED SALMON AND WATERCRESS TART

440 calories per serving Serves 6

For 25 people, multiply the quantity by four; for 50 multiply by eight; and for 100 multiply by fifteen.

225 g (8 oz) plain white flour
1.25 ml (¼ tsp) salt
1.25 ml (¼ tsp) sugar
125 g (4 oz) unsalted butter, diced
30 ml (2 tbsp) chopped fresh chives
30 ml (2 tbsp) grated Parmesan cheese
3 eggs and 2 egg yolks
225 g (8 oz) salmon fillet, skinned
125 ml (4 fl oz) white wine
freshly ground black pepper
125 g (4 oz) smoked salmon or smoked salmon trimmings
25 g (1 oz) watercress sprigs
150 ml (5 fl oz) double cream
5 ml (1 tsp) Dijon mustard

1 Sift the flour with the salt and sugar into a food processor bowl. Add the butter and process for a few seconds until the mixture looks like breadcrumbs. Add the chives and grated Parmesan.

2 Add one beaten egg. Process in short bursts until well combined. Turn the dough onto a floured surface and knead gently to bring together. Wrap in cling film and chill for at least 2 hours or overnight.

3 Place the fresh salmon in a frying pan and pour the wine over, add a sprinkle of black pepper. Bring to the boil, remove from the heat, cover and leave to cool. (The fish will cook in the cooling liquid.) Break the cold fish into large chunks, removing any bones. Roughly chop the smoked salmon and watercress.

4 Mix together with the remaining eggs, one egg yolk, cream, Dijon mustard and black pepper.

5 Roll out the pastry on a floured surface into a large rectangle about 15 x 35.5 cm (6 x 14 in). Use to line one 11.5 x 34 cm (4½ x 13½in) tranche tin (see Cook's Tip). Chill for 20 minutes in the freezer.

6 Bake the pastry case blind at 190°C (375°F) mark 5 for 15-20 minutes. Remove the baking beans and paper and cook for a further 10 minutes or until cooked and golden.

7 Brush the pastry with a little of the remaining egg yolk. Place the salmon and smoked salmon on the base of the cooked pastry case. Spoon the watercress mixture over.

8 Return to the oven on a baking sheet for 25-30 minutes or until the egg mixture is just set. Cover with foil after 10 minutes. Leave to cool for 5 minutes before cutting.

To Freeze: Complete to end of step 8. Open freeze, then wrap.

To Use: Thaw for 3 hours at room temperature. Cover with foil and reheat at 190°C (375°F) mark 5 for 10-15 minutes.

COOK'S TIP

If you do not have a tranche tin, make the tart in a 24 cm (9½ in) round fluted flan tin. Bake for a little longer, at 180°C (350°F) mark 4, covering lightly if necessary.

SPICED CASSEROLE WITH BEEF AND VENISON

275 calories per serving Serves 8

For 25 people, multiply the quantity by three; for 50 multiply by six; and for 100 multiply by eleven.

450 g (1 lb) stewing beef
450 g (1 lb) venison (see Cook's Tip)
5 ml (1 tsp) salt
5 ml (1 tsp) black peppercorns
10 ml (2 tsp) coriander seeds
150 g (5 oz) no-soak pitted prunes
150 g (5 oz) no-soak apricots
125 g (4 oz) raisins
finely grated rind and juice of 1 orange
200 ml (7 fl oz) orange juice
150 ml (¼ pint) dry sherry
450 g (1 lb) onions, skinned and finely sliced
30 ml (2 tbsp) oil
2.5 ml (½ tsp) ground mace
2.5 ml (½ tsp) ground cinnamon
pinch of allspice
15 ml (1 tbsp) flour
450 ml (¾ pint) beef stock
30 ml (2 tbsp) balsamic vinegar

1 Cut the meat into 4 cm (1½ in) cubes, then season with salt. Crush the peppercorns and coriander seeds in a pestle and mortar, or with the end of a rolling pin in a strong bowl. Soak the dried fruit in the orange juice and sherry. Cover and leave for 1 hour or overnight.

2 Heat the oil in a large flameproof casserole and brown the meat in small batches. Ensure the meat is well browned so that the casserole juices have a rich, dark colour. Add a little more oil if necessary and fry the onions until golden. Return all the meat to the pan with the spices, orange rind and flour. Cook, stirring, for 3 minutes. Add the beef stock and bring to the boil. Add the vinegar. Cover and cook at 150°C (300°F) mark 2 for 1 hour.

3 Remove the casserole from the oven. Strain the fruit and reserve. Add the soaking liquid to the casserole, to cover and cook for a further 1 hour 10 minutes or until the meats are very tender. Stir in the reserved fruits and return to the oven for 5 minutes to heat through before serving.

To Freeze: Cool, cover and freeze at the end of step 3 with fruits.

To Use: Thaw casserole overnight at cool room temperature. Add an extra 150 ml (¼ pint) beef stock, bring to boil, cover and reheat at 180°C (350°F) mark 4 for about 25 minutes.

COOK'S TIP

Supermarkets and some butchers sell stewing venison; it is also available by mail order.

ROASTED VEGETABLE PLAITS

480 calories per serving Serves 8

For 25 people, multiply the quantity by three; for 50 multiply by five; and for 100 multiply by ten.

700 g (1½ lb) mixed vegetables, such as carrot, leek, courgette, aubergine, red pepper, sweet potato, prepared
30 ml (2 tbsp) olive oil
salt and pepper
225 g (8 oz) onions, skinned and roughly chopped
2 cloves garlic, skinned and crushed
400 g (14 oz) can chopped tomatoes
15 ml (1 tbsp) sun-dried tomato paste (see Cook's Tip)
125 g (4 oz) Gruyère or Emmental cheese, grated
200 g (7 oz) mascarpone cheese
50 ml (2 fl oz) single cream
30 ml (2 tbsp) finely chopped fresh chives
50 g (2 oz) pinenuts, toasted
454 g (1 lb) packet puff pastry
1 egg, beaten
coarse salt, for sprinkling
finely chopped fresh chives, to garnish

1 Chop the mixed vegetables into 2.5 cm (1 in) chunks. Place in a small roasting tin with 15 ml (1 tbsp) olive oil and seasoning. Cook at 200°C (400°F) mark 6 for 40-45 minutes or until just tender, stirring occasionally. Remove from the oven and cool.

2 Heat the remaining olive oil in a heavy-based frying pan and fry the onions and garlic for 5 minutes or until lightly coloured. Add the chopped tomatoes and tomato paste and simmer, uncovered, for 15-20 minutes or until thick and pulpy. Set aside.

3 Mix 75 g (3 oz) of the grated cheese with the mascarpone cheese, single cream and chopped chives. Mix the vegetables with the tomato sauce, 25 g (1 oz) of the pinenuts and seasoning. Roll out the pastry quite thinly. You will need two oblongs measuring about 35.5 x 30.5 cm (14 x 12 in).

4 Beat the egg with a pinch of salt. Place half the vegetables along the centre of each oblong, about 10 cm (4 in) wide. Top the vegetables with the cheese mixture. Brush the pastry with the beaten egg.

5 With a sharp knife make diagonal incisions through the pastry about 2.5 cm (1 in) apart, down each side of the filling to within 2.5 cm (1 in) of the filling. Plait the pastry strips over the filling, making sure that the strips cross over or the pastry may burst in cooking. Tuck any loose pastry under the base. Brush liberally with the beaten egg and sprinkle with black pepper, coarse salt, remaining grated cheese and pinenuts.

6 Place the plaits on a baking sheet. Cook at 220°C (425°F) mark 7 for 25 minutes until golden brown. Cover loosely with foil if they begin to brown too quickly. Garnish with chives.

To Freeze: Open freeze and wrap at end of step 5.

To Use: Thaw for 4 hours at room temperature and cook as above for about 35 minutes or until golden brown and heated through.

COOK'S TIP

Sun-dried tomato paste is available from larger supermarkets. Alternatively, use finely chopped sun-dried tomatoes or standard tomato paste.

FRUITY MOROCCAN LAMB

540 calories per serving Serves 8

For 25 people, multiply the quantity by three; for 50 multiply by six; and for 100 multiply by eleven.

1.4 kg (3 lb) diced shoulder of lamb
10 ml (2 tsp) ground cumin
2.5 ml (½ tsp) ground cloves
10 ml (2 tsp) dried coriander
10 ml (2 tsp) dried thyme
4 medium cloves garlic, skinned and crushed
175 ml (6 fl oz) fresh orange juice
olive oil
175 g (6 oz) no-soak dried apricots
75 g (3 oz) raisins
5 ml (1 tsp) saffron threads
300 ml (½ pint) sherry
90 ml (3 fl oz) vinegar, preferably sherry vinegar
60 ml (4 tbsp) flour
600 ml (1 pint) stock, preferably lamb stock
salt and pepper
saffron rice, to accompany

1 Place the diced lamb in a bowl and add the spices, herbs and garlic. Stir well. Pour the orange juice and 45 ml (3 tbsp) olive oil over. Stir. Cover the bowl and leave the lamb to marinate in the refrigerator for at least 3 hours, preferably overnight.

2 Mix the dried apricots and raisins with the saffron, sherry and vinegar. Cover and leave to marinate at room temperature for at least 3 hours or overnight, stirring the mixture occasionally.

3 Heat a little olive oil in a large, flameproof casserole. Lift the meat from the marinade and brown in batches on a high heat. Lower heat and return all the meat to the casserole dish. Add the flour and stir well. Add the marinade, soaked fruit and its liquid and lamb stock. Season, stir well and bring to the boil.

4 Cover the casserole with a tight-fitting lid. Cook at 180°C (350°F) mark 4 for about 1 hour 15 minutes or until the meat is very tender. Accompany the lamb with saffron rice tossed with toasted flaked almonds and parsley.

To Freeze: Cool, cover and freeze casserole at end of step 4.

To Use: Thaw overnight at cool room temperature, bring to boil, cover and reheat at 180°C (350°C) mark 4 for about 40 minutes.

COOK'S TIP

Check the liquid in the casserole from time to time during cooking and top up with some extra stock if necessary.

PROVENÇAL CHICKEN BAKE

515 calories per serving Serves 8

For 25 people, multiply the quantity by three; for 50 multiply by six; and for 100 multiply by eleven.

225 g (8 oz) dried pasta shells, such as 'Orecchiette'
salt and pepper
45 ml (3 tbsp) olive oil
225 g (8 oz) onion, skinned and roughly chopped
2 cloves garlic, skinned and crushed
pinch of saffron (optional)
15 ml (1 tbsp) dried thyme
150 ml (¼ pint) dry white vermouth or white wine
two 400 g (14 oz) cans chopped tomatoes
550 g (1¼ lb) passata (see Cook's Tips)
15 ml (1 tbsp) caster sugar
700 g (1½ lb) either skinless chicken breast fillets or boned chicken thighs
25 g (1 oz) butter
25 g (1 oz) flour
450 ml (¾ pint) milk
200 g (7 oz) full-fat soft cheese
50 g (2 oz) pitted black olives
75 ml (5 tbsp) pesto sauce
basil sprigs, to garnish

1 Cook the pasta in boiling, salted water until just tender. Drain, place under cold running water and set aside.

2 Heat 15 ml (1 tbsp) of the oil in a large saucepan and cook the onions, garlic, saffron (if using) and thyme for 1-2 minutes. Pour in the dry vermouth and bubble for 2-3 minutes. Add the tomatoes, passata, seasoning and sugar. Bring to the boil and simmer for 15-20 minutes or until reduced by one third.

3 Cut the chicken into chunks. Place in a roasting tin. Drizzle over the remaining olive oil, season and cover with foil. Cook at 200°C (400°F) mark 6 for 10-15 minutes or until just cooked (see Cook's Tips).

4 Melt the butter in a heavy-based saucepan and stir in the flour. Cook, stirring, for 1 minute, then gradually add the milk and whisk until smooth. Bring to the boil, then simmer for a further 10-15 minutes, stirring occasionally. Remove from heat and whisk in the full-fat cheese and season.

5 Mix together the chicken, pasta, olives and tomato sauce and spoon into a 3.4 litre (6 pint) dish with a depth of about 4 cm (1½ in). Lightly stir the pesto into the white sauce, to create a marbled effect. Spoon the white sauce over the chicken mixture.

6 Cook at 200°C (400°F) mark 6 for 30-35 minutes or until golden brown and heated through. Serve immediately.

To Freeze: Cool, wrap and freeze at end of step 5.

To Use: Thaw overnight at cool room temperature. Cook as in step 6 for about 45-50 minutes.

COOK'S TIPS

Passata is puréed, sieved tomatoes available in bottles or cartons in most large supermarkets or delicatessens. It is perfect for pizza bases, soups and casseroles. Any left over can be frozen.

The chicken in step 3 should be just cooked. Take care not to over-cook it as it may become stringy when it is cooked a second time.

LAMB WITH ORANGE AND GINGER

800 calories per serving Serves 8

For 25 people, multiply the quantity by three; for 50 multiply by six; and for 100 multiply by eleven.

2 kg (4½ lb) leg of lamb
olive oil
450 g (1 lb) onions, skinned and finely chopped
25 g (1 oz) piece fresh root ginger, peeled and finely chopped
20 ml (4 tsp) ground ginger
30 ml (2 tbsp) flour
600 ml (1 pint) stock
125 g (4 oz) ground almonds
1 large clove garlic, skinned and crushed
4 large oranges
salt and pepper
150 ml (5 fl oz) single cream
25 g (1 oz) toasted flaked almonds
rice pilaff and green salad, to accompany

1 Cut the lamb into 4 cm (1½ in) cubes, discarding fat and bone. Heat 60 ml (4 tbsp) oil in a large flameproof casserole. Add about a quarter of the lamb and brown well. Remove from the pan using draining spoons and brown the remaining lamb.

2 Add the onions to the pan with a little more oil if necessary and lightly brown. Stir in the fresh ginger, ground ginger and flour and cook for 1-2 minutes, stirring occasionally.

3 Pour in the stock, stir in the ground almonds, garlic, grated rind of two oranges and the juice of one – about 75 ml (5 tbsp). Replace the meat, season lightly and bring to the boil. Cover tightly and bake at 170°C (325°F) mark 3 for about 1½ hours or until the lamb is very tender.

4 Peel and segment the remaining oranges, reserving any juices.

5 Take the casserole out of the oven and stir in the cream. Reheat gently on the hob without boiling, stir in the orange segments and any juices. Adjust seasoning and serve garnished with the flaked almonds. Accompany with a rice pilaff and a green salad.

To Freeze: Cool and freeze at end of step 3.

To Use: Thaw overnight at cool room temperature. Cover and reheat at 200°C (400°F) mark 6 for about 40 minutes, adding a little more stock if necessary. Complete as above.

COOK'S TIP

To prepare the day before, follow to the end of step 3. Cool, cover and refrigerate. Reheat and finish as per freezing instructions.

ROSTI-TOPPED CHICKEN AND TARRAGON PIE

530 calories per serving Serves 8

For 25 people, multiply the quantity by three; for 50 multiply by six; and for 100 multiply by eleven.

1.8 kg (4 lb) chicken
1 carrot, 2 sticks celery, ½ onion, 8 peppercorns, for flavouring
1.1 kg (2½ lb) medium old potatoes
salt and pepper
225 g (8 oz) rindless streaky bacon
1.4 kg (3 lb) leeks, cleaned
350 g (12 oz) brown-cap mushrooms
about 125 g (4 oz) butter
60 ml (4 tbsp) fresh tarragon or 30 ml (2 tbsp) dried
45 ml (3 tbsp) flour
150 ml (¼ pint) milk

1 Place the chicken and flavouring ingredients in a large saucepan. Cover with cold water and bring to the boil. Cover and simmer for about 1 hour 20 minutes or until the legs are wobbly and the juices run clear when the flesh is pierced with a skewer. Lift the chicken from the pan and cool. Reduce the stock by boiling until only 600 ml (1 pint) of liquid remains. Strain.

2 Wash the potatoes and place on a baking sheet. Cook at 200°C (400°F) mark 6 for about 50 minutes or until beginning to soften but not cooked through. Cool, peel away the skins and coarsely grate. Season.

3 Roughly chop the bacon, leeks and mushrooms (if using button mushrooms, leave whole). In a non-stick frying pan, fry the bacon on its own until crisp. Lift out of the pan and fry the mushrooms in the remaining fat for 2-3 minutes or until golden, adding a little butter if necessary.

4 In a separate saucepan, melt 50 g (2 oz) of the butter and fry the leeks with the tarragon for 4-5 minutes or until soft. Stir in the flour and cook, stirring, for 2-3 minutes before adding the reserved stock and milk. Bring to the boil, stirring all the time. Simmer for 2-3 minutes or until the sauce thickens very slightly; season and cool.

5 Remove the flesh from the chicken and chop into bite-sized pieces, discarding the skin. Stir into the cool sauce with the bacon and mushrooms and spoon into a large, shallow, ovenproof dish.

6 Place large mounds of the grated potato on top of the chicken mixture to cover completely. Melt the remaining butter and drizzle over the potato.

7 Stand the dish on a baking sheet. Cook at 200°C (400°F) mark 6 for 40 minutes or until golden and piping hot, covering lightly with foil if necessary.

To Freeze: Open-freeze, then wrap at end of step 6.

To Use: Thaw overnight at cool room temperature. Cook as directed in recipe, but increase cooking time to 1 hour.

DILL-GLAZED SALMON

290 calories per serving Serves 8

For 25 people, multiply the quantity by three; for 50 multiply by six; and for 100 multiply by eleven.

1.4 kg (3 lb) salmon or sea trout

dry white wine

onion and carrot slices, black peppercorns and bay leaf, for flavouring

1 small bunch fresh dill

2.5 ml (½ tsp) powdered gelatine

rocket or other green salad leaves and lemon and lime slices, to garnish

crisp vegetable salad and lemon mayonnaise, to accompany

---

1 Rinse the salmon well under cold running water. Remove the head and tail if wished (see Cook's Tip). Place the salmon in a fish kettle or large roasting tin. Pour over just enough cold water and a little dry white wine to cover. Add the flavouring ingredients and dill stalks. Divide the feathery dill tops into small sprigs, cover and refrigerate.

2 Cover the salmon with kettle lid or foil. Bring the liquid slowly to the boil. Simmer for 2 minutes. Turn off heat and leave the salmon (still covered) in the liquid until cold.

3 Carefully remove the salmon from the poaching liquid. Strain and reserve 150 ml (¼ pint) liquid. Carefully skin the salmon, gently scraping away any dark brown flesh to reveal the pink underneath.

4 Place the salmon on a flat serving platter. If the head and tail are still on, cut a 'v' shape into the tail to neaten it. Cover the salmon with cling film and refrigerate – at least 30 minutes.

5 Place the reserved poaching liquid in a small bowl. Sprinkle over the gelatine and leave to soak for 3-4 minutes. Place the bowl in a saucepan of simmering water and heat gently until the gelatine has completely dissolved. Cool the liquid until just beginning to thicken.

6 Brush a little of the poaching liquid over the salmon. Press the reserved dill sprigs onto the exposed salmon flesh. Brush all over with more liquid. Return to the refrigerator to set.

7 To serve the salmon, garnish with a little rocket or other green salad leaves, and lemon and lime slices. Accompany with a crisp vegetable salad and lemon mayonnaise.

To Freeze: Pack and freeze salmon at end of step 3.

To Use: Thaw overnight at cool room temperature and finish as above.

COOK'S TIPS

For a cold buffet, a salmon looks impressive with its head and tail on. If this doesn't appeal or if you don't have a fish kettle or large enough roasting tin, the salmon will still make an excellent centre-piece with the head and tail removed.

The salmon can be prepared to the end of step 6 the day before needed. For larger numbers we advise buying 1.4 kg (3 lb) salmon only and simply multiplying up the recipe. The cooking of larger salmon can be difficult as they won't fit easily into a standard fish kettle or oven.

ROAST SPICED FILLET OR SIRLOIN OF BEEF

310 calories per serving Serves 8

For 25 people, multiply the quantity by three; for 50 multiply by five; and for 100 multiply by ten.

---

1 fillet or sirloin of beef, about 900 g (2 lb)

10 ml (2 tsp) black peppercorns

75 ml (3 fl oz) oil

1 clove garlic, skinned and crushed

2.5 ml (½ tsp) salt

10 ml (2 tsp) English mustard powder

5 ml (1 tsp) ground ginger

30 ml (2 tbsp) wholegrain mustard

15 ml (1 tbsp) soft light brown sugar

oak-leaf lettuce, radicchio and fresh figs, to garnish

Herb Sauce, to accompany

---

1 Trim any excess fat or sinew from the beef. Tie with fine string at 2.5 cm (1 in) intervals. Place in a small non-metallic dish.

2 Coarsely grind the peppercorns in a pestle and mortar or put in a strong polythene bag and crush with a rolling pin. Beat together with the oil, garlic, salt,

English mustard, ginger, wholegrain mustard and sugar. Spread all over the beef, cover; refrigerate overnight.

3 Transfer the beef and marinade to a small roasting tin. Roast in the oven at 240°C (475°F) mark 9 for 20 minutes, basting occasionally. Reduce the oven temperature to 220°C (425°F) mark 7 for a further 20 minutes for medium beef or 25 minutes for well done (see Cook's Tip for sirloin cooking instructions). Remove the meat from the oven, drain off and reserve any pan juices for the sauce. Allow to cool completely.

4 With a very sharp knife, remove the string and cut the beef into wafer-thin slices. Serve on a platter of oak-leaf lettuce, radicchio and quartered figs. Serve accompanied by Herb Sauce.

Not suitable for freezing

COOK'S TIP

Fillet of beef is expensive, but when roasted in this way and thinly sliced cold, it will easily serve eight as part of a buffet. Alternatively, use the same mixture with a 900 g (2 lb) piece of boned and rolled sirloin (trim the fat and retie if necessary), but cook at 200°C (400°F) mark 6 for about 1 hour 20 minutes. The marinated beef can be cooked as in step 3 the day before it is required, then kept, covered, overnight in the refrigerator.

HERB SAUCE

225 calories per serving

Serves 8

---

200 ml (7 fl oz) olive oil

45 ml (3 tbsp) lemon juice

30 ml (2 tbsp) each chopped fresh parsley, thyme and basil

2-3 drops Tabasco sauce

any reserved pan juices from Roast Spiced Beef

salt and pepper

---

1 Blend together the olive oil, lemon juice, herbs and Tabasco sauce in a blender or food processor.

2 Skim any fat from the reserved pan juices, then whisk into the dressing. Season to taste.

Not suitable for freezing

COOK'S TIP

Any combination of herbs can be used for this recipe – choose whatever is fresh and plentiful. This combination partners the beef particularly well. It will keep, covered in the refrigerator, for up to three days, although the herbs will lose a little of their colour during that time.

BALLONTINE OF TURKEY

450 calories per serving Serves 20

Slice thinly to serve 25.
To serve 50 make 2 times recipe;
for 100 make 4 times recipe.

5.4 kg (12 lb) oven-ready turkey

butter or margarine

225 g (8 oz) onion, skinned and roughly chopped

225 g (8 oz) button mushrooms, roughly chopped

2 large cloves garlic, skinned and crushed

700 g (1½ lb) pork sausagemeat

125 g (4 oz) fresh breadcrumbs

90 ml (6 tbsp) chopped fresh parsley

60 ml (4 tbsp) Dijon mustard

grated rind and juice of 2 lemons

1 egg, beaten

salt and pepper

450 g (1 lb) smoked loin of pork (see Cook's Tips)

---

1 First bone the turkey. Place the bird breast-side down on a large chopping board. Using a small sharp knife, cut straight along the backbone. Gradually fillet the flesh away from the carcass, keeping the knife as close to the bones as possible. Take great care not to puncture the skin as it has to act as a 'case' for the turkey roast – if the skin is split, the stuffing will burst out as the joint roasts.

2 Loosen the leg and wing ball-and-socket joints with the point of the knife. Push these joints away from the carcass until they loosen and partially come away. Carefully split the leg flesh and ease out the bones and sinews. Ease out the large wing joint, reserving the small wing tips for the stock pot. Run your fingers all over the turkey flesh to ensure there are no bones or sinews remaining.

3 You should have a large oblong of skin covered with turkey meat. Remove the parson's nose. Fillet most of the leg and thigh meat from *one side* of the bird and trim any excessively fat portions of breast flesh – you should have about 900 g (2 lb) trimmed meat to freeze and use in casseroles. (It is not essential to trim this flesh, but without it the ballontine will have a better shape, with even distribution of both turkey meat and stuffing.) Cover and refrigerate the boned turkey while preparing the stuffing.

4 Heat 50 g (2 oz) butter in a sauté pan and fry the onion until beginning to brown. Increase the heat, mix in the mushrooms and garlic and fry until all excess liquid has evaporated. Stir frequently. Turn into a large bowl and cool.

5 Stir the sausagemeat, breadcrumbs, parsley, mustard, grated lemons rind and 30 ml (2 tbsp) lemon juice, the egg and plenty of seasoning into the mushroom mixture. Beat well to combine thoroughly.

6 Lay the boned turkey flat on a board, flesh side up, and spread this stuffing mixture over the flesh. Place the smoked loin (cut in half lengthways if necessary - see below) on top and then fold the turkey skin around to enclose the stuffing completely. Secure with fine skewers or cocktail sticks, or sew the skin together.

7 Spread the turkey generously with butter and season liberally with milled pepper. Wrap in foil and place in a roasting tin.

8 Bake at 180°C (350°F) mark 4 for 2½ hours. Fold back the foil and return to the oven for about 1 hour or until well browned. Test with a fine skewer; if it is cooked, the juices should run clear.

9 Lift the ballontine onto a serving plate. Either cool for about 20 minutes before slicing thickly to serve with the same accompaniments as for the Bacon-roasted Turkey (see page 94), or cool completely, cover and chill before slicing to serve.

To Freeze: To serve cold only, cool, pack and freeze once completely cold.
To Use: Thaw overnight at cool room temperature.

COOK'S TIPS

It takes time (about 30 minutes) to bone the turkey, but, fortunately, it can be done a day or two in advance; carving is then much easier. Given ample warning, however, most butchers will bone the turkey for you. Reserve all bones to make stock. The most important thing is not to puncture the skin, and to completely enclose the stuffing before roasting the ballontine. Trim away some of the turkey flesh before cooking to make a more slender version; you need enough flesh to wrap right around the pork loin. The ballontine can be pressed lightly after cooking and while cooling to make it easier to slice; we preferred not to press it to retain a well rounded joint.

Smoked loin of pork is available in the chiller cabinet of most large supermarkets. It is cooked and smoked and usually the shape of salami. If bought as a square, cut into oblongs before using as stuffing. You could use cooked ham, shaping it like a sausage.

WHITE CHOCOLATE MOUSSE TORTE

785 calories per serving Serves 12

For 25 people make 2 tortes; for 50 people make 4 tortes; and for 100 people make 7 tortes.

225 g (8 oz) ginger biscuits
125 g (4 oz) butter
700 g (1½ lb) white chocolate
600 ml (1 pint) double cream
icing sugar, cocoa powder and
Chocolate Stars, to decorate

1 Line the base of a 23 cm (9 in) round, 6.5 cm (2½ in) deep, spring-release tin with non-stick baking parchment or greaseproof paper.

2 Finely crush the biscuits. Melt 75 g (3 oz) of the butter and stir into the crumbs. Press into prepared tin and chill for 15 minutes.

3 Chop the chocolate into small pieces and place in a medium-sized saucepan with half the cream. Heat very gently, stirring occasionally, until almost smooth. Pour into a bowl and cool for 15 minutes or until just beginning to thicken, stir occasionally.

4 Whip the remainder of the cream until it forms soft peaks. Fold into the cool chocolate mixture (see Cook's Tip). Pour over the biscuit base and chill for at least 3 hours, preferably overnight.

5 Serve chilled. Remove from tin, top with Chocolate Stars and dust with icing sugar and cocoa.

To Freeze: Freeze torte in tin. When thoroughly frozen, remove, wrap and return to freezer.

To Use: Unwrap and thaw overnight in refrigerator. Decorate to serve.

COOK'S TIP

Chocolate should be barely warm but still liquid before adding the whipped cream at step 4. If the chocolate is allowed to reach too high a temperature it becomes a solid mass, but if it is too cold it won't combine with the cream.

CHOCOLATE STARS

Roughly chop 225 g (8 oz) white, plain or milk chocolate and melt with 25 g (1 oz) butter over a pan of simmering water. Spread thinly on two baking sheets lined with non-stick baking parchment and refrigerate to set. Soften at room temperature for a few seconds and stamp out star shapes; refrigerate. When the chocolate gets too soft to handle, chill again. Freeze, interleaved with non-stick baking parchment; place frozen on the torte.

GLACÉ ICING

100 calories per 25 g (1 oz)
Makes 100-175 g (4-6 oz)

125-175 g (4-6 oz) icing sugar
flavouring (optional)
colouring (optional)

1 Sift the icing sugar into a bowl, then gradually mix in 15-30 ml (1-2 tbsp) warm water until the icing is thick enough to coat the back of a spoon.

2 Stir in any flavouring. If necessary, add more sugar or water to obtain the correct consistency. Add a few drops of colouring, if required. Use at once.

NOTE

This quantity is sufficient to cover the top of a 20 cm (8 inch) cake or about 8 small cakes.

VARIATIONS

Extra-smooth Glacé Icing: Place the icing sugar, water, flavouring and colouring in a small pan and heat gently, stirring, until the mixture is warm; do not allow it to get too hot. The icing should coat the back of a wooden spoon and look smooth and glossy.

Orange or Lemon Glacé Icing: Substitute 15-30 ml (1-2 tbsp) strained orange or lemon juice for the water.

Chocolate Glacé Icing: Blend 10 ml (2 tsp) cocoa powder in a little hot water and use to replace the same amount of measured water.

Coffee Glacé Icing: Flavour with either 5 ml (1 tsp) coffee flavouring or 10 ml (2 tsp) instant coffee powder dissolved in a little of the measured and heated water.

Mocha Glacé Icing: Flavour with 5 ml (1 tsp) cocoa powder and 10 ml (2 tsp) instant coffee powder, dissolved in a little of the measured and heated water.

Not suitable for freezing

CHOUX PASTRY

575 calories per serving

Serves 4

65 g (2 ½ oz) plain or strong plain flour
50 g (2 oz) butter or margarine
2 eggs, lightly beaten

1 Sift the flour onto a plate or piece of paper. Put the butter and 150 ml (1/4 pint) water in a saucepan. Heat gently until the butter has melted, then bring to the boil. Remove the pan from the heat and immediately tip in the flour. Beat thoroughly with a wooden spoon.

2 Continue beating over a low heat until the mixture is smooth and forms a ball in the centre of the pan (take care not to overbeat or the mixture will become fatty). Remove from the heat and leave to cool for 1-2 minutes.

3 Beat in the eggs, a little at a time, adding only just enough to give a piping consistency. It is important to beat the mixture vigorously at this stage to incorporate as much air as possible. Use as recipe.

To Freeze: Wrap and freeze.
To Use: Thaw overnight at cool room temperature.

TIRAMISU GATEAU

470 calories per serving Serves 10

For 25 people make 3 gâteaux; for 50 people make 5 gâteaux; for 100 people make 8 gâteaux.

melted vegetable fat, for greasing
plain white strong flour
caster sugar
6 eggs, size 2
two 250 g (8.7 oz) tubs mascarpone cheese
5 ml (1 tsp) vanilla essence
150 ml (5 fl oz) double cream
125 g (4 oz) bar milk chocolate
125 ml (4 fl oz) cold strong black coffee
125 ml (4 fl oz) Tia Maria or any other coffee-flavoured liqueur
cocoa powder, to dust
chocolate waves, to decorate (see Cook's Tip)

1 Grease three baking sheets and dust with a little flour and sugar. Place 4 of the eggs and 175 g (6 oz) sugar in a large bowl. Whisk with an electric whisk until the mixture is pale, thick and creamy. Sift in 125 g (4 oz) flour and fold in gently.

2 Spread the mixture on the baking sheets into three circles of about 25.5 cm (10 in).

3 Bake at 200°C (400°F) mark 6 for about 10 minutes or until lightly risen, pale golden brown and firm to the touch. Cool for about 30 seconds. Loosen carefully with a palette knife and slide onto wire racks lined with non-stick baking parchment to complete cooling.

4 Meanwhile, separate the remaining 2 eggs, whisk the egg yolks with 25 g (1 oz) sugar, the cheese and vanilla essence until well blended. Fold in the lightly whipped cream and the whisked egg whites. Cover and refrigerate until required.

5 Coarsely grate the chocolate; set aside. Mix the coffee and liqueur.

6 Trim the sponges into 23 cm (9 in) rounds. Base-line a 23 cm (9 in) spring-release cake tin with non-stick baking parchment. Place one sponge round, smooth side down, in the base. Spoon over one-third of the coffee mixture. Sprinkle over half the chocolate, then spoon over half the cheese mixture. Continue layering the ingredients, ending with a sponge round, soaked in coffee mixture. Cover and refrigerate for about 5 hours, remove from the tin and refrigerate overnight.

7 To serve, dust with cocoa and decorate with chocolate waves.

To Freeze: Turn out and freeze before dusting with cocoa and decorating with chocolate.

To Use: Thaw at cool room temperature for 4 hours; complete as described above.

COOK'S TIP

To make chocolate waves, spread about 30 ml (2 tbsp) melted chocolate over the back of a baking sheet. Freeze for 1-2 minutes, then allow 20 seconds to bring to room temperature. Push the sharp edge of a wall-paper stripping knife, at an angle, into and along the chocolate, moving the blade from left to right to form large waves. Chill to set.

AMARETTO PAVLOVA

570 calories per serving Serves 8

For 25 people, multiply the quantity by three; for 50 multiply by five; and for 100 multiply by ten.

4 egg whites
125 g (4 oz) caster sugar
125 g (4 oz) soft light brown sugar
5 ml (1 tsp) malt vinegar
10 ml (2 tsp) almond essence
125 g (4 oz) granulated sugar
50 g (2 oz) flaked almonds, toasted
600 ml (1 pint) double cream
60 ml (4 tbsp) Amaretto liqueur
icing sugar, to decorate
Amaretto pears, to serve (optional)

1 Line a baking sheet with non-stick baking parchment.

2 Mix together the egg whites, caster and brown sugar in a large heatproof bowl. Place over a saucepan of gently simmering water. Do not allow the bowl to touch the water. Beat with an electric whisk for 10-15 minutes or until very stiff and shiny. Off the heat, immediately whisk in the vinegar and almond essence very quickly.

3 Pile a 23 cm (9 in) round of meringue onto the baking sheet, making sure there is a substantial hollow in the centre.

4 Bake at 110°C (225°F) mark low for about 1½ hours. Leave to cool and then carefully peel away the paper. Place on a serving plate.

5 To make the praline, place the granulated sugar in a small saucepan **DO NOT STIR** – dissolve over a gentle heat until the sugar melts and turns a golden caramel colour. Stir in the toasted nuts and pour immediately onto an oiled baking sheet. Leave until cold. Crush in a food processor or bag with a rolling pin.

6 Lightly whip the cream, stir in all but 30 ml (2 tbsp) of the praline and all of the Amaretto. Spoon into the Pavlova. Chill for about 1 hour.

7 Sprinkle with the reserved praline and icing sugar to decorate. Cut into wedges and serve with Amaretto pears, if wished.

To Freeze: Open-freeze at end of step 6. When firm, wrap and return to freezer.

To Use: Unwrap and thaw in refrigerator overnight. Complete step 7 and serve.

To Prepare Ahead: Complete the day before, cover and refrigerate.

To Serve: Toss over a high heat to heat through.

AMARETTO PEARS

Peel, halve and core four pears lengthways. Cut each half into three wedges. Melt 15 g (½ oz) butter in a non-stick frying pan and toss the pears until lightly browned, about 10 minutes. Add 45-60 ml (3-4 tbsp) Amaretto liqueur to taste, toss over a high heat for 2 minutes and serve immediately.

ICED CHRISTMAS PUDDING

454 calories per serving
Serves 8

For 25 people, make 3 puddings; for 50 make 5 puddings; and for 100 make 10 puddings.

75 g (3 oz) no-soak dried apricots
75 g (3 oz) pitted no-soak prunes
225 g (8 oz) seedless raisins, currants and sultanas, mixed
125 g (4 fl oz) brandy
450 ml (15 fl oz) double cream
4 egg yolks (see Note)
60 ml (4 tbsp) golden syrup
mango and star fruit, to decorate

1 Snip the prunes and apricots into small pieces. Place in a bowl with the remaining fruit and brandy. Stir well, cover and leave in a cool place overnight (not the refrigerator).
2 The next day, whip the cream until it just holds its shape. Whisk the egg yolks until thick and light in colour; gently warm the syrup.
3 Mix all the ingredients together in a freezer-proof container. Cover and freeze for 2-3 hours or until beginning to firm up. Meanwhile, base-line a 1.1 litre (2 pint) pudding basin with non-stick baking parchment.
4 Stir the mixture to distribute the fruit through the cream. Spoon into the basin. Cover and freeze until firm – 6-8 hours.
5 To serve, dip the basin into warm water. Loosen with a blunt-edged knife, then turn out. Serve in wedges or freeze until needed. Decorate with mango and star fruit slices.

NOTE

The young, the elderly, pregnant women and people with immune-deficiency diseases should not eat raw eggs due to the possible risk of salmonella.

FRESH FRUIT SALAD

135 calories per serving

Makes 6 servings

50 g (2 oz) sugar
juice of ½ lemon
2 red-skinned apples
2 oranges
1 small pineapple
125 g (4 oz) seedless grapes
2 bananas

1 Dissolve the sugar in 300 ml (½ pint) water. Bring to the boil and boil for 2 minutes. Cool, then add lemon juice.
2 Quarter, core and roughly chop the apples. Peel and segment the oranges. Cut the pineapple into chunks, discarding skin and core. Stir all the fruit into the syrup as it is prepared. Cover and chill for 2-3 hours.
3 Thickly slice the bananas and stir into the syrup just before serving.
Not suitable for freezing

COOK'S TIP

Choose whatever fruits you prefer; pears, kiwi fruit, mangoes, papayas etc, providing a good selection of textures and colours. You will need about two pieces of standard fruit per person. Replace the syrup with orange or grapefruit juice if preferred or add a dash of liqueur before serving.

CHOCOLATE AND ORANGE CAKE

495 calories per serving
Serves 16

For 25 people, make 2 cakes; for 50 make 3 cakes; and for 100 make 5 cakes.

oil for greasing
125 g (4 oz) white chocolate
125 g (4 oz) milk chocolate
375 g (13 oz) plain chocolate
175 g (6 oz) softened butter
175 g (6 oz) caster sugar
175 g (6 oz) ground almonds
6 eggs, size 2, separated
75 g (3 oz) fresh brown breadcrumbs
45 ml (3 tbsp) cocoa powder
grated rind and juice of 1 orange
pinch of salt
150 ml (5 fl oz) double cream

1 Grease and line a 20.5 cm (8 in) deep round cake tin. Roughly chop the white and milk chocolate.
2 Break 225 g (8 oz) plain chocolate into a bowl and melt over a pan of gently simmering water; cool slightly.
3 Beat the butter and sugar until light and fluffy. Stir in the melted chocolate with the almonds, egg yolks, breadcrumbs, cocoa, orange rind and juice.
4 Whisk the egg whites and salt to form soft peaks. Stir a quarter into the chocolate mixture; fold in the remainder with the chopped chocolate. Pour into the prepared tin.
5 Bake at 180°C (350°F) mark 4 for about 1 hour 40 minutes, covering loosely with foil if necessary. Cool in the tin for 15 minutes before turning out onto a wire rack.
6 Place the remaining 150 g (5 oz) plain chocolate and cream in a bowl. Melt over a pan of gently simmering water, stirring occasionally. Cool for about 30 minutes or until slightly thickened. Pour over the cake to cover. Cool and store in an airtight container for up to five days.

To Freeze: Pack and freeze at end of step 5.
To Use: Thaw, wrapped, for 5 hours

Wedding Cake

325 calories per slice
Makes about 125 slices

COOK'S TIP

Serving quantities are given for each cake, it is up to you whether you want to provide two or three tiers.

---

375 g (13 oz) seeded raisins, such as lexia

250 g (9 oz) glacé cherries

200 g (7 oz) shelled almonds

550 g (1¼lb) seedless raisins

450 g (1 lb) currants

700 g (1½lb) sultanas

250 g (9 oz) chopped candied peel

250 g (9 oz) ground almonds

105 ml (7 tbsp) brandy

175 g (6 oz) plain chocolate, in pieces

700 g (1½ lb) butter or margarine

700 g (1½lb) soft dark brown sugar or muscovado sugar

---

finely grated rind of 3 large lemons

13 eggs

800 g (1 lb 12 oz) plain white flour

7.5 ml (1½ tsp) ground cinnamon

7.5 ml (1½ tsp) grated nutmeg

60 ml (4 tbsp) black treacle

TO MATURE:

105 ml (7 tbsp) brandy

TO COVER:

Apricot Glaze (see page 137)

about 1.9 kg (4½ lb) Almond Paste (see page 139)

about 1.9 kg (4½ lb) Fondant Icing (see page 139)

TO DECORATE:

about 450 g (1 lb) Royal Icing (see page 140)

SUGAR-PASTE FLOWERS:

about 450 g (1 lb) petal paste

---

lemon-yellow dusting powder

about 72 white stamens (double-headed)

TO FINISH:

ribbon or board edging

fresh flowers

---

1 Use 15 cm (6 in), 20 cm (8 in) and 28 cm (11 in) round, deep cake tins. Line the three cake tins with a double thickness of greaseproof paper. Tie a double thickness band of brown paper around the outside of the tin. To mix the ingredients for all three cakes together, use a very large bowl. Alternatively you may find it easier to mix the cakes separately (see chart for quantities).

2 Prepare the fruit and nuts: chop the seeded raisins; wash, dry and halve the cherries; blanch and shred the almonds. In a large bowl, mix these together with the seedless raisins, currants, sultanas, peel, ground almonds and brandy.

Wedding Cake Quantities

Ingredients	15 cm (6 inch) round	20 cm (8 inch) round	28 cm (11 inch) round
seeded raisins (lexia)	50 g (2 oz)	125 g (4 oz)	200 g (7 oz)
glacé cherries	40 g (1½ oz)	60 g (2½ oz)	150 g (5 oz)
whole almonds	25 g (1 oz)	50 g (2 oz)	125 g (4 oz)
seedless raisins	75 g (3 oz)	175 g (6 oz)	300 g (11 oz)
currants	50 g (2 oz)	125 g (4 oz)	275 g (10 oz)
sultanas	125 g (4 oz)	200 g (7 oz)	375 g (13 oz)
chopped candied peel	40 g (1½ oz)	60 g (2½ oz)	150 g (5 oz)
ground almonds	40 g (1½ oz)	60 g (2½ oz)	150 g (5 oz)
brandy	15 ml (1 tbsp)	30 ml (2 tbsp)	60 ml (4 tbsp)
plain chocolate	25 g (1 oz)	50 g (2 oz)	75 g (3 oz)
margarine/butter	75 g (3 oz)	200 g (7 oz)	400 g (14 oz)
soft dark brown sugar	75 g (3 oz)	200 g (7 oz)	400 g (14 oz)
lemons	½	1	2
eggs	1½	4	7½
plain white flour	150 g (5 oz)	225 g (8 oz)	425 g (15 oz)
ground cinnamon	1.25 ml (¼ tsp)	2.5 ml (½ tsp)	3.75 ml (¾ tsp)
grated nutmeg	1.25 ml (¼ tsp)	2.5 ml (½ tsp)	3.75 ml (¾ tsp)
black treacle	7.5 ml (1½ tsp)	15 ml (1 tbsp)	30 ml (2 tbsp)
ALMOND PASTE	350 g (12 oz)	550 g (1¼ lb)	1 kg (2¼ lb)
FONDANT ICING	350 g (12 oz)	700g (1½ lb)	1 kg (2¼ lb)

3 Melt the chocolate in a heatproof bowl over a pan of simmering water; allow to cool.

4 In a separate bowl, cream the butter, sugar and lemon rind until pale and fluffy. Add the eggs one at a time, beating well.

5 Sift the flour with the spices. Fold half carefully into the creamed mixture. Add the other half to the fruit; mix well and add to the creamed mixture with the chocolate and treacle. Stir.

6 Divide the mixture among the three tins, taking care to make the largest cake slightly deeper than the others.

7 Bake the two small cakes together first. Spoon the cake mixture into the large tin, cover and put in a cool, dry place until ready to cook. Bake at 150°C (300°F) mark 2 for the first hour, then reduce to 140°C (275°F) mark 1. Cook the small cake for a further 1-1½ hours, the medium cake for a further 1½-2 hours and the large cake 3½-5 hours longer. (If the cakes are cooked together they will take considerably longer.) After 2 hours' cooking, cover with greaseproof paper. Cool in the tins, then transfer to wire racks.

8 Pierce the cakes at regular intervals with a fine skewer, spoon a little brandy over each and leave for several hours to soak in. Wrap in greaseproof paper, then overwrap with foil and leave to mature in a cool, dry place for 1-3 months, impregnating with a little brandy at regular intervals.

9 Cover the cakes with almond paste.

10 Cover the cakes with fondant icing.

APRICOT GLAZE

55 calories per serving
Makes 150 ml (¼ pint)

125 g (4 oz) apricot jam

1 Place the jam and 30 ml (2 tbsp) water in a small pan. Heat gently, stirring, until the jam begins to melt. Bring to the boil and simmer for 1 minute.

2 Strain the jam through a nylon sieve. Use while warm.

ALMOND PASTE

135 calories per 25 g (1 oz)
Makes 450 g (1 lb)

225 g (8 oz) ground almonds
125 g (4 oz) caster sugar
125 g (4 oz) icing sugar
1 egg
5 ml (1 tsp) lemon juice
5 ml (1 tsp) sherry
1-2 drops vanilla essence

1 Place the ground almonds, caster sugar and icing sugar in a bowl and mix together. In a separate bowl, whisk the egg with the remaining ingredients and add to the dry mixture.

2 Stir well to mix, pounding gently to release some of the oil from the almonds. Knead with your hands until smooth.

COVERING A CAKE WITH ALMOND PASTE

For recommended quantities, see the chart on page 138.

You will need to make up a quantity of Apricot Glaze before applying the almond paste.

1 If the cake has an uneven top, cut it level. Turn the cake over so the flat bottom becomes the top. Sift some icing sugar onto a clean work surface.

2 Roll out half the almond paste slightly larger than the top of the cake. Using the cake tin as a guide, cut the paste to fit. Brush the top of the cake with warm apricot glaze.

3 Lift the almond paste onto the cake and smooth over, neatening the edges. Place on a cake board, which should be 5 cm (2 in) larger than the cake.

4 Cut a piece of string the same height as the cake with its almond paste top, and another to fit around the side of the cake. Roll out the remaining almond paste and, using the string as a guide, trim the paste to size. Brush the sides of the cake and the almond paste rim with apricot glaze.

5 Roll up the almond paste strip loosely. Place one end against the side of the cake and unroll to cover the sides of the cake. Use a palette knife to smooth over the sides and joins of the paste. Flatten

the top lightly with a rolling pin. Leave the cake in a cool, dry room to dry out thoroughly for about two days before applying the icing.

FONDANT ICING

95 calories per 25 g (1 oz)
Makes about 450 g (1 lb)

400 g (14 oz) icing sugar
1 egg white
50 g (2 oz) liquid glucose
(available from chemists)

1 Sift the icing sugar in a large bowl. Make a well in the centre and add the egg white and glucose. Beat these ingredients with a clean wooden spoon, gradually pulling in the icing sugar.

2 When the mixture becomes stiff, turn onto a surface sprinkled with icing sugar. Knead thoroughly to a smooth paste.

3 If necessary, store tightly wrapped in cling film in a cool place.

COOK'S TIP

Fondant icing – or moulding icing – provides an easy to apply covering. It is also used to mould decorations. Ready-to-roll icing (ready-made fondant) is used in the same way.

COVERING A CAKE WITH FONDANT ICING

For recommended quantities, see the chart on page 138.

1 First, cover the cake with almond paste and allow to dry. Sprinkle a clean work surface with cornflour and dredge your rolling pin. Roll out the icing until it is 12-15 cm (5-6 in) larger than the cake top.

2 Supporting the icing on a rolling pin, place it centrally over the top of the cake, allowing the icing to drape over the sides. Press the icing onto the sides of the cake.

3 Work it with your hands sprinkled with cornflour or icing sugar, from the centre of the cake; gently ease the icing down the sides to give an even covering.

4 Trim excess icing from the base. Smooth icing, using a circular movement with the fingers. Leave for about two days to dry before decorating.

ROYAL ICING

100 calories per 25 g (1 oz)
Makes 450 g (1 lb)

2 egg whites or albumen powder equivalent

10 ml (2 tsp) liquid glycerine

450 g (1 lb) icing sugar

1 If using the egg whites with the glycerine, place them in a bowl and stir just enough to break up the egg whites. If using albumen powder, mix according to manufacturer's instructions.

2 Using a clean wooden spoon, add a little sieved icing sugar and start mixing very gently.

3 Add a little more icing sugar as the mixture becomes lighter. Continue to add the sugar, stirring gently but thoroughly until the mixture is stiff and stands in soft peaks. If required for coating, it should form soft peaks; for piping it should be a little stiffer.

4 Transfer the royal icing to an airtight container, cover the icing closely with cling film to exclude air and prevent the surface of the icing drying out, then seal. When required, stir the icing slowly.

COOK'S TIP

Omit the glycerine from the recipe if the icing is to cover a tiered cake, as a hard surface is required to support the tiers.

FLAT ICING A CAKE WITH ROYAL ICING

Always apply royal icing over a layer of almond paste.

1 Put a large spoonful of icing onto the centre of the cake and spread out, using a palette knife in a paddling motion; this helps to eliminate air bubbles.

2 Draw an icing ruler across the top of the cake towards you, applying an even pressure and keeping the ruler at an angle of about 30°. Remove surplus icing by running a palette knife around the edge, at right angles to the cake.

3 To cover the sides, for best results, place a round cake on a turntable. Spread icing onto the sides using the same paddling motion. Hold a cake scraper at an angle of about 45° and draw it around the side, then pull it off quickly to leave only a slight mark. Dry in a cool place for 24 hours. Store the remaining icing as above.

4 The next day, scrape away any rough icing from the top edge with a small sharp knife. Clean fine sandpaper can be used to achieve a very smooth finish. Brush off loose icing with a clean pastry brush. Apply two or three further coats, allowing each coat to dry overnight before applying the next. Leave to dry overnight before applying decorations.

COOK'S TIP

Allow approximately 450 g (1 lb) royal icing to elaborately pipe a 30 cm (12 in) cake.

TO DECORATE THE CAKE

To make 24 sugar-paste azaleas and 180 cut-out flowers, you will need the following special equipment: a set of three blossom cutters, with ejector; small and medium 5-point calyx cutters; medium 8-petal daisy cutter; set of rose-petal cutters; a sponge block, a ball modelling tool and fine paintbrushes.

Making Small Flowers

1 Break off a piece of sugar paste about the size of a large pea. (Keep the remaining paste tightly covered to prevent it from drying out.) Roll out the paste as thinly as possible using a little cornflour or icing sugar (the thinner it is, the better the flower).

2 Using the blossom, calyx and daisy cutters, cut out flowers. The blossom cutters with ejector are easiest to use – depress the plunger over the sponge and the paste is automatically cupped in the shape of a flower. For the cutters without ejectors, use the ball modelling tool to cup the paste; leave to dry.

3 Knead a little yellow dusting powder into some of the sugar paste. Repeat as above until you have about 180 flowers in all. When dry, pipe a small dot of royal icing into the centre of each flower. Dry.

Making Azaleas

4 Roll out a small piece of yellow sugar paste very thinly, keeping the rest well covered. Cut out five petals, using the large rose-petal cutter.

5 Gently mark the centre vein of each petal with a cocktail stick and two veins on either side. Create the frilled edge by gently rolling a cocktail stick along the curved edge of the petal. Place the petal against a wooden spoon handle to curve into shape. Repeat with the remaining four petals.

6 Line two to three large piping nozzles with foil. Brush one side of the petal with water; place the next petal in position, overlapping the edges. Repeat until all five petals are in position, using the nozzles to hold in shape; dry. Repeat using various cutters until you have twelve large, six medium and six small azaleas.

7 Dust the outside of the flowers lightly with the lemon colour. Dampen a fine brush with water and paint small spots of dust inside each azalea. Pipe a dot of royal icing into the centre of each flower. Cut three stamens in half to give six heads, cut to size and position in the icing. Leave to dry.

Applying Decorations

8 Make the templates: cut a strip of paper to fit around the side of each cake. Fold into six equal portions. Cut out a semi-circle making sure the folds are linked. Transfer the outline using pin pricks.

9 Using the pin pricks as a guide, attach the sugar-paste flowers with a dot of royal icing. Attach one or two azaleas on top of the cake where each loop forms a point. Attach two small cut-out flowers to neaten the back of the azaleas.

10 Using a No 14 star or No 5 rope nozzle, pipe shells of royal icing along the bottom edge of each cake.

TO ASSEMBLE THE CAKE

You need eight round 7.5 cm (3 in) hollow cake pillars and eight wooden skewers for assembling – in situ, of course. Mark the position of the pillars on the bottom two tiers of the cake. Place in position and insert the skewers carefully into the cake until the point reaches the cake board. Mark the skewers 3 mm (⅛ in) above the top of the pillar. Remove and cut them to size. Replace the skewers and assemble the cake. Finish with flowers.

Index